# The Books of History

CONCORDIA PUBLISHING HOUSE · SAINT LOUIS

3558 S. Jefferson Ave., St. Louis, MO 63118-3968
1-800-325-3040 • cph.org



Illustrations by Barbara Kiwak



Portions of this book have been compiled from, adapted from, and inspired by various sources, including *The Lutheran Study Bible*, Concordia Publishing House, 2009; the Concordia Commentary series, Concordia Publishing House, 1996–; *Lutheran Bible Companion*, vol. 1, Concordia Publishing House, 2014; and *Concordia's Complete Bible Handbook for Students*, Concordia Publishing House, 2011.



Manufactured in China

1 2 3 4 5 6 7 8 9 10 33 32 31 30 29 28 27 26 25 24

# TABLE OF CONTENTS

# Welcome

Welcome to *Guiding Word*. This six-volume collection will help you better read and understand the Bible, the most important book ever written. In it, we read and hear God's Word, which is written so that we may believe that Jesus is the Christ, and that by believing we may have eternal life in His name (John 20:31).

Why have another Bible resource? First, the Bible is a complex library of books, and it is often intimidating for people to read on their own. Second, while there are many resources designed to help you read and understand the Bible, each has its own format and style and may not be suitable for every learner. We hope this resource will fill a gap and be useful for you.

Think of this series of books as a travel guide to the Bible. Just as a travel guide helps you prepare for and better enjoy a trip, this resource will enable you to better understand and appreciate the Bible as you journey through it. The sections have been designed to help you prepare for reading and understanding difficult passages, to explain the overall course of the Scriptures, to prompt you to reflect on the text as you read, to point out important milestones and events, and to guide you to Jesus' presence throughout the Bible.

If you are already familiar with the organization of the Bible, feel free to skip ahead to the section titled "What's in *Guiding Word*?"

## What's in the Bible?

The Bible is all about God's plan to restore fallen humanity and His broken creation by sending His Son. But what's in the Bible? How do we look at it? How do we use it? Though we call the Bible a book, it's actually a collection of sixty-six books. These were written over a period of 1,500 years by many authors.

The Bible has two divisions: the Old Testament and the New Testament. We don't use the word *testament* too often today. It's related to words like *covenant* and *contract*.

The Old Testament includes the first thirty-nine books of the Bible. These are the books written about the events that happened before Jesus was born. They all point us toward Jesus. The name *Old Testament* is a little misleading because sometimes we think of old things as not important or out of style. Instead, these books can be thought of as the first covenant or promise that God made to His people to send the Savior, Jesus. And as you will see, Jesus is present throughout the Old Testament. The New Testament includes the last twenty-seven books of the Bible, which record Jesus' life and mission, as well as the life of Jesus' early followers in the church. These books point us back to Jesus and how He fulfilled all of God's promises made for us in the Old Testament. Again, these are all about Jesus.

The books of the Bible are organized in a way that may seem confusing at first but makes sense when you know the system. How are the books in a library organized? In libraries, books are organized by their type. Fiction is in one section, and nonfiction is in another; magazines are in one spot and children's books in another. The same goes for the Bible. Instead of the books being ordered by the date they were written or by their authors, the books of the Bible are put in categories, or genres; then the books are generally organized by date written within that genre.

## Navigating the Library

The first five books of the Old Testament—Genesis, Exodus, Leviticus, Numbers, and Deuteronomy—are called the Books of Moses, or the Torah, meaning "Law of God." They were written down by Moses and are covered in the first volume of this series.

The next books in the Old Testament are called the Books of History. These tell the history of God's people from the time of Moses up to the time of Jesus and are covered in the second volume.

Next are the Books of Wisdom and Poetry. These poetical books were written at different times during the Old Testament history, mostly by kings David and Solomon. These are covered in the third volume.

The last group of Old Testament books are the Books of the Prophets. These books record God's special messages to His Old Testament people, mostly during the second half of their history. They are discussed in the fourth volume.

The New Testament has five genres. The first four books—Matthew, Mark, Luke, and John—are called the Gospels. Each Gospel tells of the life and mission of Jesus from a different writer and perspective. These accounts make up the heart of the Bible and are covered in the fifth *Guiding Word* volume.

Next is the book of the Acts of the Apostles (also known simply as Acts). This historical book records events from the early years of the Christian Church and the lives of the first Christians after Jesus ascended into heaven. The next books are called the Pauline Epistles (*epistle* means "letter"). These are letters that the apostle Paul wrote to the early Christians. Near the end of the New Testament are the General Epistles. These are letters that other people besides Paul wrote to the early Christians. The final book of the Bible is the only book of prophecy in the New Testament, the book of Revelation. This shows the vision Jesus revealed to the apostle John about life in the end times (that is, the time between Christ's first and second coming) and the restoration of God's creation. The books of Acts through Revelation are covered in the sixth and final volume of *Guiding Word*.

### 66 BOOKS OF THE BIBLE

|  |  |
|---|---|
| **OLD TESTAMENT** | GENESIS |
| BOOKS OF MOSES *(Torah)* | EXODUS |
| | LEVITICUS |
| | NUMBERS |
| | DEUTERONOMY |
| HISTORY | JOSHUA |
| | JUDGES |
| | RUTH |
| | 1 SAMUEL |
| | 2 SAMUEL |
| | 1 KINGS |
| | 2 KINGS |
| | 1 CHRONICLES |
| | 2 CHRONICLES |
| | EZRA |
| | NEHEMIAH |
| | ESTHER |
| WISDOM & POETRY | JOB |
| | PSALMS |
| | PROVERBS |
| | ECCLESIASTES |
| | SONG OF SOLOMON |
| PROPHETS | ISAIAH |
| | JEREMIAH |
| | LAMENTATIONS |
| | EZEKIEL |
| | DANIEL |
| | HOSEA |
| | JOEL |
| | AMOS |
| | OBADIAH |
| | JONAH |
| | MICAH |
| | NAHUM |
| | HABAKKUK |
| | ZEPHANIAH |
| | HAGGAI |
| | ZECHARIAH |
| | MALACHI |
| **NEW TESTAMENT** | MATTHEW |
| GOSPELS | MARK |
| | LUKE |
| | JOHN |
| HISTORY | ACTS |
| PAULINE EPISTLES *(Letters)* | ROMANS |
| | 1 CORINTHIANS |
| | 2 CORINTHIANS |
| | GALATIANS |
| | EPHESIANS |
| | PHILIPPIANS |
| | COLOSSIANS |
| | 1 THESSALONIANS |
| | 2 THESSALONIANS |
| | 1 TIMOTHY |
| | 2 TIMOTHY |
| | TITUS |
| | PHILEMON |
| GENERAL EPISTLES | HEBREWS |
| | JAMES |
| | 1 PETER |
| | 2 PETER |
| | 1 JOHN |
| | 2 JOHN |
| | 3 JOHN |
| | JUDE |
| END TIMES | REVELATION |

### Navigating the Bible

When you open up a Bible, you'll see chapter and verse numbers scattered throughout the pages. Did you know that those numbers were not originally there? As people used the Bible more and more and made copies, later scholars eventually put in these numbers to help people quickly find sections or passages. We call these Bible references.

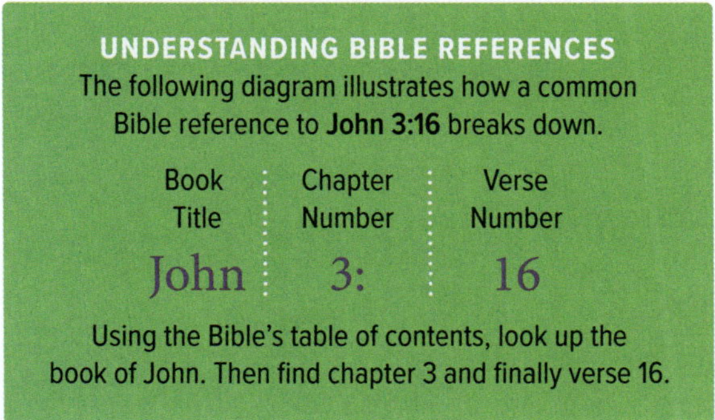


## What's in *Guiding Word*?

Each volume of *Guiding Word* is laid out in a similar fashion. After this series introduction is an introduction for that specific volume. Then, each book of the Bible has its own introduction, which will help you better understand and dig into that particular book.

Each book of the Bible follows an outline, which breaks the book into major divisions and then each division into sections. The section heads were not included in the original biblical text but were added later to help clarify how the text flows from narrative to narrative or idea to idea. In *Guiding Word*, these correspond to the subheadings in the ESV translation of the Bible. From here on out, we will refer to these subhead sections as "passages."

Following the pattern of a travel guide, *Guiding Word* includes some features to help you read through, better understand, and reflect on each passage of the Bible. These features include the following:

(1) **Orientation.** This is a short summary of each passage. Just as a travel guide gives you a glimpse of where you will be going on your journey before you arrive, the summary will help orient you to where you are in the Bible and where you are going. After reading the summary for each passage, read the text itself in your Bible. Alternatively, if you are skimming a book of the Bible, previewing the book, or only want to understand the high points before reading deeper, these summaries are a good place to start.

(2) **Observation Points.** In the side margins, you will find open-ended questions. Use these reflection questions to help you slow down, observe, and reflect on the passage. There is room in the side margin for recording reflections, thoughts, and notes as you go. Just as a travel guide will prompt you to look out for specific things on your way, the reflection questions will help you better observe what's going on in the text.

**(3) Landmarks.** These special features, interspersed in the text, will help you appreciate the overall journey through God's Word. In any journey, you will encounter landmarks of all types that pop out to you, may interest you, or may even make you scratch your head. Landmarks in *Guiding Word* are identified by icons and colored bars, and can be read before or after you read the corresponding passage. Landmarks include the following categories

### VISUALIZE

This feature includes maps, diagrams, pictures, or infographics to help you visualize scenes, locations, and concepts in a passage.

### PICTURE OF THE SAVIOR

This Old Testament feature highlights people, places, or events that set the stage for the coming of Jesus and help reveal His work of salvation.

### LINK BETWEEN THE TESTAMENTS

In the Old Testament, this Landmark highlights people or events that Jesus or His apostles will discuss, explain, or fulfill in the New Testament. In the New Testament, this feature points the reader back to the Old Testament person or event that set the stage for the New Testament passage.

### CLEAR THE CONFUSION

This Landmark clarifies passages that are likely to leave the reader confused and fills the gaps—providing backstories, describing future developments, or discussing the significance of the event.

### SET THE SCENE

This feature explains important cultural or historical themes that help you better understand the context of the passage.

### WAYPOINT

This feature is designed to be a longer stopping point. When you travel, you will likely stop at notable locations for an extended period of time to really experience the destination. Waypoints in *Guiding Word* function like stopping points that are worth investigating along the journey through God's Word. Each Waypoint has a three-part structure:

- What does this text show us?

- What does this text reveal about God's plan of salvation?
- What does this text uncover about our identity and calling as God's people today?

Each Waypoint also has reflection questions associated with it. The Waypoints can be considered on your own or in a group study. However you choose to use the Waypoints is up to you, but use the summaries and reflection prompts to help guide you through a deeper reading of the text.

## How to Use *Guiding Word*

You can use this resource in multiple ways:

- Read through the Bible on your own, passage by passage. The summary of each passage will help orient you to where the narrative is taking you, and the reflection questions are observation prompts that will help you pay closer attention to what you're reading. The interspersed Landmark features will help you visualize important images or concepts, or understand and connect key themes to the overall story of the Scriptures.
- Read through the Bible in a small group or Bible study setting. The guided summaries and reflection questions make good prompts if you are reading through the Scriptures as a group, providing some reflections along the way. The Waypoint sections also serve as great places to stop and reflect on key narratives.
- Read a good thirty-thousand-foot summary of the Bible. *Guiding Word* includes summaries of passages, and if you have never read certain books of the Bible or are intimidated by their length, you can take a few minutes to get introduced or oriented to them via summaries and graphics.

Whether or not you've read through all or parts of the Bible before, *Guiding Word* will serve as your companion and guide through the journey.

## The Books of History

The twelve Old Testament books that follow the Books of Moses trace God's dealings with Israel after Moses' death. Covered are the conquest of the Promised Land; the four hundred years of the judges; the united kingdom under Saul, David, and Solomon; and the divided kingdoms of Israel and Judah, which ended with exile and the return of a remnant of Judah.

These books show us God's faithfulness despite His people's unfaithfulness. God sends prophets, faithful judges, and kings to deliver His people from their enemies. But evil kings, faithless priests, and lying prophets lead God's people into worshiping false gods and abandoning the Lord their God. Finally, after the people of Judah are conquered and exiled for seventy years in Babylon, God brings them back to the Promised Land to rebuild the temple and await the birth of the Child first promised to Adam and Eve so many years before.

## Journeying through the Books of History

These twelve Books of History teach us much not only about God's grace, mercy, and patience but also about His holiness and vengeance. The book of Joshua describes the conquest of the Promised Land. Judges describes the sad downward spiral of God's people as they abandoned Him over and over, even though God had raised judges to deliver them. The book of Ruth focuses on one family God had preserved from extinction and chosen as He extended the line from Adam and Eve to the promised Christ. The books of 1 and 2 Samuel relate Israel's demand for a king and the first two kings God had provided for Israel, including David, the most famous ancestor of the Christ.

The books of 1 and 2 Kings relate the disintegrating reign of David's son Solomon, which ultimately led God to divide the kingdom into two. Despite many faithless kings ruling both kingdoms, God faithfully sent His prophets, until He had to punish the ever-increasing wickedness of His people with captivity. The books of 1 and 2 Chronicles retrace the history of God's people from the very beginning, then focus especially on the descendants of King David, the importance of Solomon's temple, and the temple's destruction by the Babylonians.

The last three historical books highlight the return of Judah's exiles to rebuild the temple in Jerusalem and await the birth of God's Son. Ezra describes how God returned the exiles to Jerusalem and helped them overcome great challenges and opposition in order to rebuild the temple and restore worship. Nehemiah describes the rebuilding of the walls of Jerusalem through which God protected His people and made them secure from the threats of their enemies. Finally, Esther recounts how God saved His people from annihilation. Israel's twisting and turning history not only warns us of the dangers of the enemies who surround us but also reminds us that our God is faithful to protect and deliver us.

These books are filled with great suspense, but there are a few difficult passages—like the first nine chapters of 1 Chronicles, with their endless genealogical lists, or the early chapters of Ezra, with their comprehensive listing of the returned exiles. Though it may at times feel like you are reading a phone book, remember that God knew each of the individuals behind these obscure names. They were all dear to Him, and no joy, worry, or fear escaped His careful, watching eye. Through all of human history, His burning desire has been and still is to save all people through the life, death, and resurrection of David's promised Son, our Savior, Jesus Christ. That includes the countless unnamed saints from Adam and Eve to Christ's return whose life stories have been lost to history—even you and me.

### The Books of History, with Their General Divisions

- **Joshua**
  - The Lord Prepares Israel to Inherit the Land (1:1–5:12)
  - Israel Captures the Land (5:13–12:24)
  - The Lord Allots the Land to Israel (13:1–21:45)
  - Israel to Live in the Land (22:1–24:33)
- **Judges**
  - Prologue to the Period of the Judges (1:1–2:23)
  - The Judges Cycle (3:1–16:31)
  - The Dual Epilogue (17:1–21:25)

- **Ruth**
  - The Dilemma (1:1–22)
  - The Hope (2:1–23)
  - The Risk (3:1–18)
  - The Solution (4:1–22)
- **1 Samuel**
  - The Birth and Calling of Samuel (1:1–3:21)
  - The Ark and the Lord's Presence (4:1–7:2)
  - Changing Leadership (7:3–12:25)
  - King Saul's Crisis (13:1–15:35)
  - Saul and David (16:1–31:13)
- **2 Samuel**
  - David Becomes King of Judah (1:1–4:12)
  - David Becomes King of All Israel (5:1–10:19)
  - David's Sin and Family Troubles (11:1–18:33)
  - David Is Restored and Completes His Reign (19:1–24:25)
- **1 Kings**
  - David's Reign Ends (1:1–2:12)
  - Solomon's Reign and Disobedience (2:13–11:43)
  - Division of the Kingdom of Israel and Jeroboam's Reign (12:1–14:20)
  - Kings of Israel and Judah and the Prophet Elijah (14:21–22:53)
- **2 Kings**
  - Jehoram's Reign in Israel and the Prophet Elisha (1:1–8:15)
  - Kings of Israel and Judah Until Israel's Defeat and Captivity (8:16–17:41)
  - Judah's Last Kings (18:1–24:20)
  - Judah's Fall and Exile (25:1–30)
- **1 Chronicles**
  - Nations and Israel in God's Plan of Salvation (1:1–9:34)
  - The Establishment of David's Reign and the Centrality of the Ark of the Covenant (9:35–17:27)
  - David's Military Campaigns (18:1–20:8)
  - David Prepares for Location and Building of the Temple (21:1–22:19)
  - David Organizes Temple Worship (23:1–26:32)
  - David Leaves the Kingdom to Solomon (27:1–29:30)
- **2 Chronicles**
  - History of Solomon and Building of the Temple (1:1–9:31)
  - Division of the Kingdom of Israel (10:1–12:16)
  - The Davidic Dynasty Before the Assyrian Invasion (13:1–26:23)
  - Invasions and the Fall of the Davidic Dynasty (27:1–36:23)
- **Ezra**
  - First Return of Exiles and Rebuilding of the Temple (1:1–6:22)
  - Second Return of Exiles Under Ezra (7:1–8:36)
  - Ezra's Reforms Ban Intermarriage (9:1–10:44)
- **Nehemiah**
  - Nehemiah's First Visit and Rebuilding of Jerusalem's Walls (1:1–12:47)
  - Nehemiah's Second Visit: Problems and Solutions (13:1–31)
- **Esther**
  - Threat to Judeans (1:1–5:14)
  - Deliverance of Judeans (6:1–10:3)

# JOSHUA

## Welcome to Joshua

The book of Joshua begins with the people of Israel camped on the banks of the Jordan, preparing to cross into the Promised Land. The book of Joshua shares its name with the lead character and author, Joshua the son of Nun. Before dying, Moses had commissioned Joshua to lead the children of Israel. Now Joshua receives God's directions as he leads the people across the Jordan River and into the land promised to their ancestor Abraham.

What are your first impressions of the book of Joshua? What narratives or images come to your mind when you reflect on this book? What are specific things you'd like to learn more about?

## Joshua at a Glance

- **Start:** Following the death of Moses, Joshua takes on the leadership of the children of Israel as they prepare to enter the Promised Land.
- **End:** The book of Joshua ends with the death of Joshua as the people settle into everyday life in the Promised Land.
- **Theme:** God guides His people to take possession of the land He had promised to Abraham.
- **Author and Date:** Joshua, and perhaps others, wrote this book between 1406 and 1375 BC.
- **Places Visited:** The Jordan River, Jericho, Shiloh, and other places in the Promised Land
- **Journey Time:** The twenty-four chapters of Joshua can be read in about one hour and forty-five minutes.
- **Outline:**
    - The Lord Prepares Israel to Inherit the Land (1:1–5:12)
    - Israel Captures the Land (5:13–12:24)
    - The Lord Allots the Land to Israel (13:1–21:45)
    - Israel to Live in the Land (22:1–24:33)

## Five Top Sights and Spectacles of Joshua

**Crossing the Jordan River (3:1–17)** Walk with the Israelites across the dry riverbed of the Jordan and enter into the Promised Land.

**Circumcision and Passover Renewed (5:1–12)** Celebrate with the tribes of Israel as they renew the covenant of circumcision and remember God's mercy in the Passover.

**Conquering Jericho (5:13–6:27)** Hear the trumpet blast and the sound of crumbling walls as God's power brings down the mighty walls of Jericho.

**The Sun Stands Still (10:1–15)** Shade your eyes from the sun, which stops moving across the sky as the Lord gives His people extra daylight to complete their victory.

**Settling the Land (13:1–21:45)** Follow along as each of the tribes learns the location of the land they will occupy.

## Seeing Jesus in Joshua

The name *Joshua* means "the Lord saves," the same name the Greek New Testament records as *Jesus*. Joshua's life and service among the children of Israel reflect the life and ministry of Jesus among all nations. Jesus gives His own life to forgive the sins of all people and drives out our enemies so that we might inherit the land He has promised in the new heavens and the new earth.

## The Lord Prepares Israel to Inherit the Land (1:1–5:12)

God makes final preparations for Israel to cross the Jordan and inherit the land He promised to Abraham, Isaac, and Jacob. God commissions Joshua, a Canaanite woman protects two spies, Israel crosses the Jordan River, and the Israelites are circumcised and celebrate their first Passover in the Promised Land.

When is a time you've longed to hear God's encouragement to "be strong and courageous"?

### God Commissions Joshua (1:1–9)

Following the death of Moses, God commissions Joshua to lead His chosen people into the Promised Land. In this commission, God repeatedly encourages Joshua with the words "Be strong and courageous" (vv.

6–7, 9) as He lays out the plan to give the people a land of their own. Like Joshua, we can trust in God's promise to be with us wherever we go (see v. 9).

## Joshua Assumes Command (1:10–18)

Joshua sends the leaders out among the people, telling them to prepare their provisions because within three days they will cross the Jordan into the land promised to them by God. Trusting God to protect the families they leave behind, the bold warriors from the tribes of Reuben, Gad, and half of Manasseh set out with their brother Israelites. The troops promise their loyalty to Joshua as their new leader.

## Rahab Hides the Spies (2:1–24)

Joshua sends two men to spy on Jericho and the surrounding territory. The spies find lodging in the house of Rahab, a prostitute. When the king of Jericho demands that Rahab turn over the spies, she sends the king's men to search the countryside while she hides the spies on her roof.

Rahab tells the spies that the men of Jericho are terrified by God's great deeds for Israel. Confessing faith and trust in the true God of Israel, she asks the spies to protect her and her extended family when the Israelites return to capture the city. The men instruct Rahab to hang a red cord from her window in the city wall and promise to keep her family safe when the Israelites come to destroy Jericho. Trusting in their promise, Rahab lowers the men from the window, and they escape.

Consider the risks Rahab took in hiding the Israelite spies. When you look back in history, what other times have individuals or groups defied their governments because it was the right thing to do?

**CLEAR THE CONFUSION**

**Why did the spies choose the home of Rahab the prostitute?**

While Rahab was a prostitute, the spies did not come for her professional services. Because of her occupation, two strangers did not stand out from other men in the house. Rahab's house was built into the city wall, providing a quick escape for the spies.

Rahab reported that the people of Jericho remembered God's great deeds for Israel in Egypt and at the Red Sea and were terrified. She recognized the power and greatness of the true God and chose Him over the gods of Jericho.

## VISUALIZE

### The Promised Land

The Promised Land was far from empty; the Canaanites fully occupied the land. But God would deliver thirty-one kings into Joshua's hand.

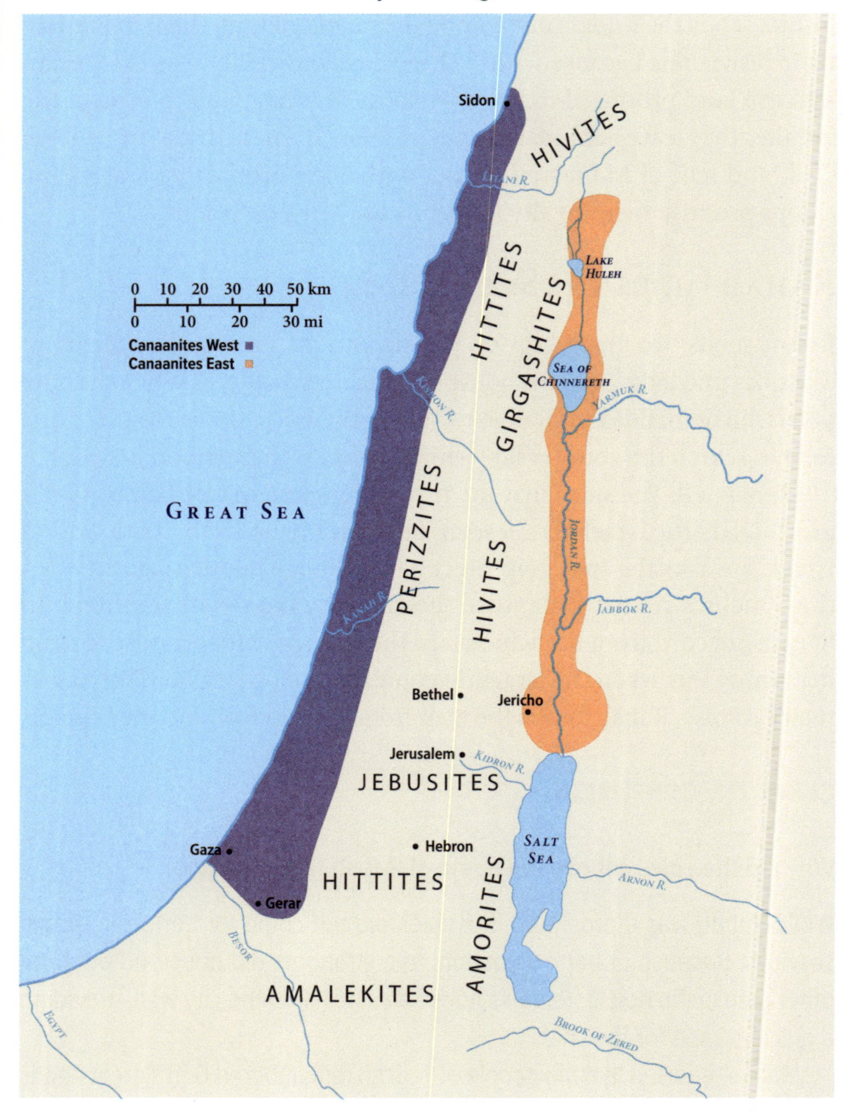


## PICTURE OF THE SAVIOR

### Rahab Risked Her Life for the People of Israel

Rahab risked hiding the spies even though the king was alerted to their presence. In His great mercy, God included Rahab in Christ's bloodline. Just as Rahab risked her life to protect the spies, her descendant Jesus laid down His life for our sake when we didn't deserve it and were unlovable by all accounts, showing the greatest love of all by dying to atone for our sins.

## Israel Crosses the Jordan (3:1–17)

### WAYPOINT

***What does this text show us?***
Joshua tells the people to keep their distance from the ark of the covenant. The priests take up the ark and, when they step into the flooded Jordan, the waters pile up, leaving dry ground for the people to cross. The ark remains until all the people pass safely to the other side.

***What does this text reveal about God's plan of salvation?***
Forty years earlier, God opened a dry path through the waters of the Red Sea. Now He brings Israel into the Promised Land through the waters of the Jordan River. One day, His own Son—the promised Savior—will be baptized in these waters as He begins His public ministry.

***What does this text uncover about our identity and calling as God's people today?***
Our heavenly Father washes away our sins as we pass through the waters of Holy Baptism. Through Baptism, our sins are cleansed and we are made new, ready to serve God through our vocations.

Review the details of this Bible account. What things cause you to marvel at the work of our God?

Think about a time when you witnessed a Baptism—perhaps one of your children or another family member. What do you recall about that experience? How did you see God at work in that event?

How does God use you in service to others?

### CLEAR THE CONFUSION

**Why did the God of love demand the destruction of the Canaanites?**

The Canaanites were descendants of Noah's son Ham (Genesis 10:15–19). Ham's descendants were cursed after he dishonored his father in Genesis 9:24–25. The Canaanites lived between the Mediterranean Sea and the Jordan River.

The seven nations of Canaan each rejected God's grace. They practiced child sacrifice, divination, sorcery, occult practices, and sexual depravity. In mercy, God brought Abraham, Isaac, and Jacob to sojourn among them and declare His message of repentance and salvation. Despite these three generations living in their midst, the Canaanites continued to defy God.

## Twelve Memorial Stones from the Jordan (4:1–24)

Joshua assembles a stone memorial in the river where the priests stood with the ark. He sends one man from each tribe to pick up a stone from the dry riverbed and carry it to the shore where he will assemble a memorial to remind future generations of what God had done at that place.

### VISUALIZE

**Memorial Stones**

The two stone memorials erected in and alongside the Jordan River were reminders of God's work in that place. We see similar stone memorials in Genesis 28:18, at the place where Jacob had dreamed of a stairway stretching to heaven; in Genesis 35:14, at the place God had met with Jacob and changed his name to Israel; and in Genesis 35:20, to mark Rachel's tomb.

What event in your life so transformed everything that it could be marked with a memorial for your future generations to remember?

## The New Generation Circumcised (5:1–9)

When the Canaanite kings hear God has brought the Israelites across the flooded Jordan, "their hearts melted" (v. 1) with dread. The Lord orders Joshua to circumcise the men born in the wilderness, as they renew the covenant established with Abraham.

### CLEAR THE CONFUSION

**Why did God command a second circumcision?**

Evidently the faithless first generation of Israelites had neglected to circumcise their sons born during the forty years in the wilderness. Having crossed into Canaan, Joshua gathered all of these men and circumcised them.

## First Passover in Canaan (5:10–12)

Israel had only celebrated two Passovers, the first in Egypt and the second a year later in the desert. Now they celebrate for the first time in the Promised Land. The next day, the manna ceases. From this point they will eat the produce of the land of Canaan.

After a forty-year lapse, the Israelites once again celebrated the Passover. What special celebrations do you look forward to? How do you celebrate special occasions with your family?

# Israel Captures the Land (5:13–12:24)

In this section, Joshua meets the commander of the armies of the Lord, who will defeat the Canaanites. Jericho falls, Joshua fights the kings of central Canaan, and Joshua defeats kings in southern and northern Canaan.

## The Commander of the LORD's Army (5:13–15)

As Joshua views Jericho, he encounters a man with a drawn sword. The man identifies Himself, "I am the commander of the army of the Lord" (v. 14). Joshua falls on his face before the man.

### PICTURE OF THE SAVIOR

**The Commander of the Lord's Army**

In other places in the Scriptures, angels take on the appearance of humans to deliver messages or protect God's people. However, the man's order to Joshua to take off his shoes because he is on holy ground points to a different identity.

When Moses approached God in the burning bush, he was told to remove his shoes because he was on holy ground. Angels do not make the ground holy; only God's presence does. So, Joshua encountered the Son of God in His preincarnate state as the commander of the Lord's army.

## The Fall of Jericho (6:1–27)

### WAYPOINT

***What does this text show us?***

Israel marches around Jericho once each day for six days. On the seventh day they march seven times around the city, raise their voices in a shout, and God breaks down the walls. The Israelites go straight in and kill all the people of Jericho.

Rahab and her family are rescued by the spies whom she had sheltered in her

The people of Jericho trusted in their walls to protect them. What things are you sometimes tempted to trust in?

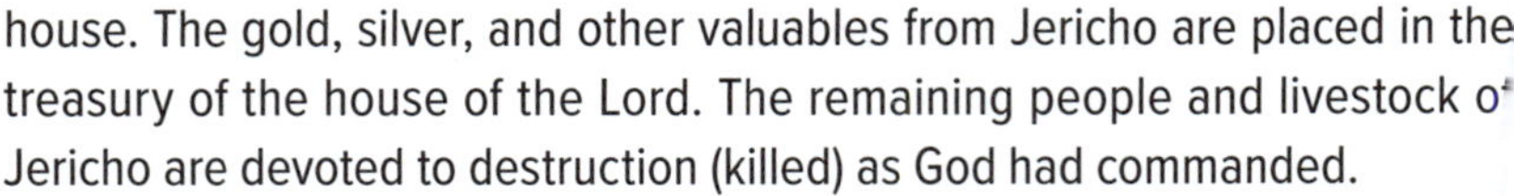

house. The gold, silver, and other valuables from Jericho are placed in the treasury of the house of the Lord. The remaining people and livestock of Jericho are devoted to destruction (killed) as God had commanded.

The residents of Jericho put their trust in their walls, but their stones were no match for God's power. What kinds of walls do we foolishly construct? How does God break down the walls in our hearts?

***What does this text reveal about God's plan of salvation?***
God gives victory to His people through a seemingly impossible method. His rescue of Rahab and her family from the complete destruction of Jericho points ahead to God's deliverance of His people from the final destruction of all creation. When Christ returns, He will take all believers to Himself, while the unbelievers will suffer eternal condemnation.

How does the assurance of salvation given to you in Christ help you live your life every day?

***What does this text uncover about our identity and calling as God's people today?***
In Christ, we will be rescued from the threat of eternal death and destruction. At the Last Day, our heavenly Father will remove all evil from His creation and we will live with Him forever in the new heavens and the new earth.

## Israel Defeated at Ai (7:1–9)

When the people send spies to evaluate the next city, Ai, the Israelites decide that they only need a small band of fighting men to go up against it. When Israel goes up against the forces of Ai, they suffer great loss of life. Joshua falls on his face in dismay before the Lord.

## The Sin of Achan (7:10–26)

Consider Achan's response to being confronted by Joshua. How do you react when confronted with your own sin?

God tells Joshua to address the sin of the people. As Joshua draws lots, God reveals that an Israelite named Achan has taken a cloak, silver, and gold from Jericho that belonged to God. Achan's family and livestock are taken to the Valley of Achor, where the people stone them to death.

**PICTURE OF THE SAVIOR**

**Priestly Leaders**

While he was not a priest, Joshua's approach to Achan was both priestly and pastoral. Rather than coming with threats of violence, Joshua called him "son" and offered Achan the opportunity to confess his sin. Joshua sought Achan's repentance and to give glory to God the Father.

## The Fall of Ai (8:1–29)

God tells Joshua to make another assault against Ai. This time, they will ambush the overly confident enemies. God allows the soldiers to plunder the possessions of the city for themselves. Tragically, if Achan had waited one more battle, he could have taken possession of the Canaanite plunder with God's blessing.

## Joshua Renews the Covenant (8:30–35)

Following the victory against Ai, Joshua builds an altar to God and offers sacrifices of burnt offerings to Him. Joshua reminds the people of their commitment to the Law by rereading all that Moses had written for them and their posterity.

## The Gibeonite Deception (9:1–27)

In a desperate ploy to avoid the fate of Jericho and Ai, the Canaanites in Gibeon successfully fool Israel, who fail to seek God's counsel. Saving their lives through their successful deception, the Gibeonites are servants of the lowest class but still alive among God's people.

## The Sun Stands Still (10:1–15)

**WAYPOINT**

***What does this text show us?***
Five kings from central Canaan combine their military might to attack Gibeon for its covenant with Israel. God fights valiantly for Israel and even grants Joshua's prayer to make the sun stand still high in the sky to give Israel the time to complete the rout of its enemies.

***What does this text reveal about God's plan of salvation?***
God sends Joshua to rescue the Gibeonites from the attack by the Canaanite kings and even suspends the laws of nature to provide daylight to complete the battle. When Christ Jesus hung on the cross, God miraculously made the sun stop shining in the middle of the day, providing a miraculous victory over our enemies of sin, death, and the devil.

***What does this text uncover about our identity and calling as God's people today?***
Though the Gibeonites were not part of God's covenant with the Israelites, He still protects them since the Gibeonites have allied themselves with His people. They foreshadow God's acceptance of Gentiles in the New Testament church. As His witnesses in the world today, we can share the message of His love for all nations through His Son, Jesus Christ.

The Canaanite kings thought they could combine forces to defeat God's army. How did God help His people defeat their enemies?

How did the darkness on Good Friday testify to what God was doing through His Son's suffering and death on the cross?

## Five Amorite Kings Executed (10:16–28)

During Israel's complete victory over the Canaanite forces, Joshua traps five kings in a cave, leaving guards to prevent their escape. Then, after overthrowing their cities, he returns to execute each of them in obedience to God's command.

## Conquest of Southern Canaan (10:29–43)

Having defeated Jericho, Ai, and five kings in central Canaan, Joshua records God's conquests in the southern region of Canaan. In each case, he fully commits to each city's destruction, and God delivers him and the Israelite forces through each endeavor.

### CLEAR THE CONFUSION

**What was divine warfare like during Israel's conquest?**

Divine warfare was the instrument God wielded to destroy Satan's hold over mankind. The Lord used divine warfare to punish the sins of the unfaithful Canaanites. At the same time, He showed His chosen people His continuing love and care for them. Through Israel, God will send His Son, Jesus, to achieve the final and complete victory over death and Satan through His death and resurrection.

## Conquests in Northern Canaan (11:1–23)

In a familiar scene, the northern kings band together in an attempt to repel Israel, but Joshua leads Israel to overwhelming victory by God's direction once again. After the main forces fall, Joshua swiftly captures and destroys the cities of Canaan's northern region.

## Kings Defeated by Moses (12:1–6)

Joshua sums up the complete Canaan campaign, including the Canaanite kings Sihon and Og, who had been overthrown under Moses' leadership. These territories east of the Jordan River had already been given to the tribes of Reuben and Gad and the half-tribe of Manasseh.

## Kings Defeated by Joshua (12:7–24)

Next, Joshua lists the thirty-one kings on the west side of the Jordan River who fell by God's hand while he led the Israelites.

# The Lord Allots the Land to Israel (13:1–21:45)

In this section, Joshua lists the land still to be conquered. He records the land each tribe will inherit, describing portions both east and west of the Jordan River, and lists the towns each tribe must allot to the priests and Levites.

## Land Still to Be Conquered (13:1–7)

God crushed the might of the Canaanites and gave Israel the core of Canaan. Now He identifies what land remains in Canaanite hands. As the Israelites continue to increase and multiply in the coming generations, God promises to be with them and drive out these remaining enemies.

Why do you suppose Joshua takes the time to list the territories that the people have yet to conquer? How does planning for the future, even if we are not part of that future, prove helpful for the church overall?

## The Inheritance East of the Jordan (13:8–33)

Joshua describes the inheritance of each Israelite tribe. He opens with a general overview of the lands Moses allotted to Reuben, Gad, and one half of Manasseh on the eastern side of the Jordan River.

## The Inheritance West of the Jordan (14:1–5)

Joshua identifies the division of all lands west of the Jordan River. He reminds them they may be divided geographically, but all the tribes of Israel are to remain one people.

## Caleb's Request and Inheritance (14:6–15)

**VISUALIZE**

**Ready for Battle**

Joshua allots Hebron as a special inheritance to Caleb, who, along with Joshua, had been one of the faithful spies who first explored the Promised Land forty-five years earlier (Numbers 13). The aged Caleb set out to win his inheritance with God's help. (His nephew Othniel will be Israel's first judge and deliverer in Judges 3.)

How did Caleb demonstrate both incredible patience and trust as he laid claim to the promise made years before? When have you needed to demonstrate extreme patience and trust?

## The Allotment for Judah (15:1–63)

Judah receives the first and largest share of land because Jacob's three older sons had forfeited this inheritance by their sins. (Reuben slept with Rachel's servant, Bilhah, in Genesis 35:22, and Simeon and Levi murdered the men of Shechem in Genesis 34:25–26.) From this tribe will come the promised Savior.

Tribal allotments were divided between families and became the inheritance passed down from generation to generation. Does your family have any property that has been handed down from generation to generation?

## The Allotment for Ephraim and Manasseh (16:1–17:18)

The two tribes from the sons of Jacob's favored son, Joseph, are allotted lands. The tribe of Ephraim, the descendants of Joseph's second son, is the first to receive land as ordained in Genesis 48:17–20. Both tribes share in the double portion of material blessing.

## Allotment of the Remaining Land (18:1–10)

Further plans are necessary to divide the rest of the land among the seven remaining tribes. Joshua leads them through the next stages of the allotment process to ensure they follow God's promises unto completion.

**SET THE SCENE**

**Shiloh**

The seven remaining tribes gathered at Shiloh as Joshua divided the unallocated territory among them. Shiloh lies about twenty miles north of Jerusalem in the heart of the Promised Land. The tent of meeting was set in Shiloh, which served as the center of worship for the Israelites for the next three hundred years.

## The Inheritance for Benjamin (18:11–28)

The first lot drawn was for the tribe of Benjamin. Their land inheritance was small but would become the hot spot and central point for many of the nation's most important events.

## The Inheritance for Simeon (19:1–9)

The second lot went to the tribe of Simeon. Their allotment was located within the large territory of Judah as a result of Jacob's curse on Simeon, but the land was a blessing for many years to come.

## The Inheritance for Zebulun (19:10–16)

Zebulun won the third lot. This tribe set up camp west of the Sea of Chinnereth (called the Sea of Galilee in Jesus' time). Their descendants would be the first recipients of the Gospel from Jesus.

## The Inheritance for Issachar (19:17–23)

Issachar claimed the fourth lot. Their land lay just south of Zebulun's, and their southern border ran neatly along the Kishon River.

## The Inheritance for Asher (19:24–31)

Asher received the fifth lot. This land ran along the coast of the Mediterranean up to Sidon and encompassed Tyre. God gave the responsibility of a politically and religiously hostile border territory to a tribe that would falter in holding firm against the tides of conflict.

## The Inheritance for Naphtali (19:32–39)

The sixth lot fell to Naphtali. The location along the northern border would expose them to much strife over the years, but it would also position them to be some of the first to hear the Gospel of Christ years later.

## The Inheritance for Dan (19:40–48)

Dan received the seventh and final inheritance. Because of their unfaithfulness, however, they never claimed these cities (Judges 1:34). In the alternative home they found far to the north, they would soon be overrun by pagan worship (Judges 18).

Tribal allotments and inheritances that stayed in families for generations gave a sense of permanence to the Israelites. How can this help you picture eternal life with Christ in the new heavens and earth?

## VISUALIZE

### Allotments for the Twelve Tribes of Israel

**SET THE SCENE**

**Joppa**

The Bible first names the city of Joppa here in Joshua 19:46. Joppa is located atop a high hill just south of the modern city of Tel Aviv, overlooking the Mediterranean. Hiram, king of Tyre, will raft cedar and pine timbers down to Joppa for the construction of Solomon's temple. Likewise, the people of Phoenicia will ship lumber here to build the second temple.

Jonah 1:3 lists Joppa as the city from which Jonah attempted to sail to Tarshish. In the New Testament, Joppa is named in Peter's missionary work as the home of both Tabitha (Dorcas), whom Peter raised from the dead, and Simon the tanner (Acts 9:36–10:23).

### The Inheritance for Joshua (19:49–51)

After the tribes receive their allotment, it is Joshua's turn. As a reward for his faithful spying alongside Caleb, he also receives what he had requested from God: just one city, Timnath-serah.

### The Cities of Refuge (20:1–9)

As Moses commanded, Joshua appoints the cities of refuge. These six shelters are placed so that all Israelites will be close to a refuge in the case of unintentional manslaughter. Those who knowingly commit murder will still be subject to punishment.

### Cities and Pasturelands Allotted to Levi (21:1–45)

The Levites are scattered across many cities throughout the nation to serve as priests and teachers of God's people.

## Israel to Live in the Land (22:1–24:33)

In this final section, Joshua dismisses the eastern tribes to return to the land beyond the Jordan River. Joshua gives his farewell, and Israel renews its covenant with the Lord.

During the conquest under Joshua, the eastern tribes awaited the end of the war before they could return and enjoy their inheritance. In what ways are our earthly lives similar to their war years?

### The Eastern Tribes Return Home (22:1–9)

Since the eastern tribes fulfilled their promise to fight alongside their brothers, Joshua releases them back to their homes east of the Jordan. He charges them to share the wealth and goods they have won with their families and, more importantly, to continue walking in God's commandments.

## The Eastern Tribes' Altar of Witness (22:10–34)

### VISUALIZE

**Altar to God**

The Transjordanian tribes build a large altar to God at the Jordan River on their way home from Joshua's conquests. The rest of Israel interprets this act as a departure from their centralized faith at the tabernacle. Envoys from these tribes reassure them that they did not build this altar for sacrifice but for a witness so future generations in Canaan will not disinherit their brothers living across the Jordan. This provision for the future looks to the coming of the promised Savior.

## Joshua's Charge to Israel's Leaders (23:1–16)

### WAYPOINT

***What does this text show us?***
Joshua delivers his farewell sermon to God's people, reminding them of God's great faithfulness and admonishing them to hold fast to His Commandments in the face of foreign idolatry. God's promises for both His beloved people and His enemies are sure to be fulfilled, says Joshua, so remain in Him.

***What does this text reveal about God's plan of salvation?***
Like Moses before him, Joshua reminds the people to remain loyal to the Lord's covenant. God has brought them through warfare and now gives them a time of rest. This rest anticipates the eternal Sabbath rest that will be ours through the life, death, and resurrection of our Savior, Jesus Christ.

***What does this text uncover about our identity and calling as God's people today?***
Joshua repeatedly warns the people against unfaithfulness and idolatry. He warns people of all ages of the destruction coming at the end of the world. Through Jesus' death and resurrection, we are saved from the final judgment

Review the Bible text for this section. How does God remain faithful to us even when we experience suffering?

How does our Sabbath rest assure us of God's care?

What kinds of things does God warn His faithful people against?

and made part of the Body of all believers. As His holy nation, we can serve others and share the message of Christ with others in our world today.

## The Covenant Renewal at Shechem (24:1–13)

At Shechem, Joshua reviews the story of salvation by grace from Abraham to the present time. He recalls God's continued love toward Israel even when they turned away or disobeyed His will most egregiously.

## Choose Whom You Will Serve (24:14–28)

**WAYPOINT**

***What does this text show us?***
Joshua leads Israel in a bold confession of faithfulness to God, our Redeemer. They promise to serve Him alone and to put away both the old idols of Egypt and the new idols of their unfamiliar home.

***What does this text reveal about God's plan of salvation?***
Joshua reminds the people that God drove out all their enemies before them. Though they promise to follow and trust in God alone, they cannot do so on their own. God has chosen them and gives them the ability to follow Him through His grace and mercy, which is shown to all believers.

***What does this text uncover about our identity and calling as God's people today?***
On our own, we cannot follow God or trust in His love and care for us. Instead, we depend totally on His grace and mercy, shown to us through the person and work of Jesus Christ. In Christ, we receive forgiveness for our sins, and through the Spirit, we are strengthened for daily living as God's children.

How and where can we make a bold confession of faith?

Consider the choice with which Joshua challenges the people: "Choose this day . . ." (24:15). How would most people in our world respond? How would you and your family respond?

How can we respond to God's grace and mercy shown to us in the person and work of Jesus Christ?

## Joshua's Death and Burial (24:29–33)

When Joshua dies his body is laid to rest in his own inheritance. Likewise, the bones of the patriarch Joseph and the body of the high priest Eleazar are buried in their respective inheritances, as Israel enters a new era of God's faithfulness.

# JUDGES

## Welcome to Judges

What do you know about the book of Judges? What are some specific things you'd like to learn more about?

The book of Judges chronicles a roughly three-hundred-year period in Israel's history between the conquest under Joshua and the monarchy of Saul. As God's people settle into the land He had first promised to Abraham, their spiritual state follows a predictable pattern. Again and again, they worship foreign idols, and God subjects them to oppression by their neighbors for a time. Over and over, this oppression brings the people to repentance. They cry out to God, and He raises up a leader who saves them from their enemies. These leaders, or judges, are tribal chieftains from different areas of the Promised Land. They represent a broad swathe of people, with varying levels of faithfulness to God. Regardless of who they are, God uses them as His instruments to deliver His people. Sadly, after each judge dies, the people wander away from God yet again.

Marvel at God's faithfulness to His people, despite their moral and spiritual decay. Dive in to read, reflect upon, and consider God's people during the three centuries of history outlined in Judges.

## Judges at a Glance

What kinds of leaders has God raised up in your church? How about in your government? Which of them led you closer to God? Which tried to pull you away from Him?

- **Start:** Judges begins at the time of the death of Joshua and the elders of Israel between 1399 and 1375 BC.
- **End:** The narrative in Judges ends with Samson's death around 1049 BC. The book itself concludes with five chapters of epilogue, which likely happened earlier but are placed at the end of the book to maintain the core theme.
- **Theme:** Judges presents Israel's declining spiritual state after the initial settlement in the Promised Land and the Lord's mercy by which He forgave them and sent them leaders to hold them together.
- **Author and Date:** Though the author is not known for certain, the prophet Samuel likely wrote Judges around 1000 BC.
- **Places Visited:** The tribal divisions and cities throughout the Promised Land

- **Journey Time:** The twenty-one chapters of Judges can be read in just over an hour and a half.
- **Outline:**
    - Prologue to the Period of the Judges (1:1–2:23)
    - The Judges Cycle (3:1–16:31)
    - The Dual Epilogue (17:1–21:25)

## Five Top Sights and Spectacles of Judges

**Israel's Unfaithfulness and God's Response (2:11–23)** Observe how God's people fall into the temptation to serve false gods and bring on themselves great pain and destruction. Marvel as God faithfully raises up tribal leaders to save them from their enemies.

**Ehud the Assassin (3:12–30)** See how God raises up an unlikely assassin to deliver God's people from the tyrannical oppression of the Moabites.

**Deborah, Barak, and Jael (4:1–5:31)** Discover how God raises up two women to overthrow and overcome the advances of the Canaanites, despite the cowardice and unfaithfulness of the male leaders.

**Gideon (6:1–8:35)** Watch as God patiently raises up an unlikely leader to deliver His people from an alliance of nomadic invaders. Scrutinize this leader as he uses shrewd and often brutal ruling strategies, falling further and further from God's ideal leader.

**Samson (13:1–16:31)** Examine Samson's extraordinary journey to single-handedly defeat Israel's Philistine oppressors. Rejoice as God uses this deeply sinful and flawed man to deliver His people.

## Seeing Jesus in Judges

Judges details the ongoing corruption and spiritual decay of God's people. Yet there is a hopeful thread throughout: God is faithful to His promise and raises up saviors who deliver His people. These deeply flawed judges foreshadow the ultimate Savior, Jesus Christ. God would one day raise up Jesus, who would save us from the powers of sin, death, and hell.

Throughout Judges' narratives, God is guiding toward this epic destiny by preserving and sustaining His people despite their idolatry and sin. In fact, the Angel of the Lord—the Second Person of the Trinity before He was born into flesh—appears several times in the book of Judges. Notably, the Angel of the Lord appears to warn the people of their sin and the consequences it would bring upon them (chapter 2), as well as to prophesy the birth of Samson to his parents (chapter 13). All along, Christ is present with His people, who await the day when He would be born to deliver us from sin and death.

# Prologue to the Period of the Judges (1:1–2:23)

In this first section, Israel has conquered the core of the Promised Land but fails to drive out the remaining Canaanites and worships their false gods and idols. These first two chapters establish the tumultuous pattern of God's people as they live their first centuries in the Promised Land.

## The Continuing Conquest of Canaan (1:1–26)

After Joshua's death, the individual tribes begin to drive out the Canaanites who are still living in the territories allotted to the tribes. Judah and Simeon have initial success, as does Joseph's tribe of Ephraim.

## Failure to Complete the Conquest (1:27–36)

Though the Israelite tribes grow strong, they fail to completely expel all the Canaanites who remain and worship false gods. Instead, they permit some foreigners to live alongside them.

**What were the consequences of failing to complete the conquest?**

Though Joshua led Israel to break the power of the Canaanites, the conquest was not completed. The coming generation should have completed the conquest but instead chose to enslave some inhabitants and live alongside others. The foreign neighbors of the Israelites worshiped false gods and continually influenced God's people to false worship.

What are some dangerous evil influences you tolerate in your life? What consequences could come from not conquering them with Jesus' help?

## Israel's Disobedience (2:1–5)

The Angel of the Lord, who was likely the preincarnate Christ, appears to the people of Israel and announces to them that the inhabitants will be a thorn in their side and a snare to them because they have failed to remove the idol worshipers from their land. The people weep bitterly.

## PICTURE OF THE SAVIOR

### The Angel of the Lord

The Angel of the Lord is a mysterious figure in the Old Testament. God often sent spirit messengers (the word *angel* means "messenger") to pass along His communications to people in the Old Testament.

The Angel of the Lord, however, was different. Not only did this Angel have a special title but He also spoke directly as God Himself. Throughout church history, this Angel has been rightly identified as the Second Person of the Trinity, the Son of God, before He put on human flesh as Jesus. When God communicated directly with His people in the Old Testament in a form they could see and hear within the bounds of creation, that was likely another appearing of the Angel of the Lord. In this case, the same Angel who appeared to Joshua before the conquest (Joshua 5:13–15) now appeared to the people after the first campaign, warning them against failure to complete the task and against idolatry. The Angel of the Lord, God Himself, would one day take on human flesh to win the final victory over sin, death, and the devil in our place on the cross.

## The Death of Joshua (2:6–10)

Joshua dies, and there is great mourning. God's people now have no central leader. Instead, within the period of the judges (the time between Joshua and Saul), God raises up local chieftains, or judges, as needed.

## Israel's Unfaithfulness (2:11–15)

As prophesied, God's people soon fall to worship the foreign idols of the surrounding people. This passage outlines the cycle the Israelites fall into throughout the time of the judges and well beyond. First, because the Israelites fail to heed the Lord's warning, God's anger burns against them, and then God allows neighboring peoples, whom He has previously held at bay, to invade and subdue His people.

How is the pattern of sin, repentance, and redemption at the time of the judges similar to the daily life of the Christian today? How is it different?

## The LORD Raises Up Judges (2:16–3:6)

Next in the cycle, God's people call out to God for deliverance. He hears their prayers and raises up a chieftain from one of the tribes. God uses this judge to deliver His people from their subjugation and to lead them back to proper worship of God. When the judge dies, the people quickly revert to idolatry. This cycle dominates the book of Judges.

**The Judges Cycle**

Many accounts in the book of Judges follow a similar pattern: God's people enjoyed prosperity, they fell away to worship false gods, they were oppressed, they cried out to God for rescue, and He provided a savior judge who delivered them from their distress. This pattern is similar to our lives of daily sin, the need for repentance, and forgiveness in Christ. We can learn from this pattern to avoid sins that lead us away from God and also rejoice that God in Christ is our eternal deliverer from sin and death.

# The Judges Cycle (3:1–16:31)

The bulk of this book outlines the many judges whom God raises up to deliver His people. Though not perfect, the first few leaders demonstrate a great level of trust in God and His ability to deliver His people. Each judge throughout the book, however, successively drifts further from the ideal, generally displaying less trust in God's power. Regardless, God uses them to do His work despite their weakness.

## Othniel (3:7–11)

After God's people worship the Baals and the Asheroth, the idols of Canaan, they are subjugated by the king of Mesopotamia. God raises up Othniel (the nephew of Caleb, the faithful spy and champion of God's people) to deliver them. The Israelites have peace for forty years.

### CLEAR THE CONFUSION

**What are the Baals and the Asheroth?**

The Canaanites' chief god was Baal, with his wife Asherah (the plural form for *Asherah* is *Asheroth*). They are referred to as Baals and Asheroth because they were local gods worshiped in many different locations. Baal worshipers sacrificed to Baal and his wife because they falsely believed it would improve the fertility of their crops.

## Ehud (3:12–30)

### VISUALIZE

Again God's people rejected the Lord, and were conquered by Eglon the king of Moab. The Moabites were descendants of a son of Lot, Abraham's nephew (Genesis 19:30–38). God raised up an unlikely judge, the left-handed Ehud of the tribe of Benjamin, who assassinated Eglon, escaped, and led God's people to victory over the Moabites. They had peace for eighty years.

?

Ehud relied on treachery, deception, and murder to deliver Israel. When have you used ungodly methods to accomplish something?

### CLEAR THE CONFUSION

**Isn't assassination wrong?**

Murder violates God's good will for His people. In fact, many of Ehud's methods, including deception, treachery, and assassination, are not ones that Christians today should imitate. Nonetheless, God raised up Ehud to deliver His people from oppression. God raised up many such people for His purposes in the

Scriptures. We are to follow God's will as told in His Word and trust God to work all things for our good as we seek to follow His ways in our lives.

## Shamgar (3:31)

God also raises up Shamgar, who not only delivers God's people from the Philistines but does so in spectacular fashion by killing six hundred of them with an oxgoad (a long, pointed stick, used to prod cattle).

## Deborah and Barak (4:1–24)

### WAYPOINT

***What does this text show us?***
The people again do great evil in God's sight and He delivers them into the hands of Jabin, king of Canaan, for twenty years. God raises up Deborah, a prophetess, to call God's people to war. When the military leader Barak refuses to lead the battle without Deborah, she joins him. God's people win the battle, and when the Canaanite general runs away, God uses the cunning of another woman, Jael, to assassinate him.

***What does this text reveal about God's plan of salvation?***
God desired men to lead His people, especially in times of war. But when men were unwilling to lead, God raised up not one but two women to deliver His people. If God makes a promise, He will keep it, despite the lack of trust of His people. In a similar way, this is what Jesus has done for us. Despite our lack of faith, He is faithful and just to deliver us because of His promise. He has done so by the unusual means of the cross and His resurrection.

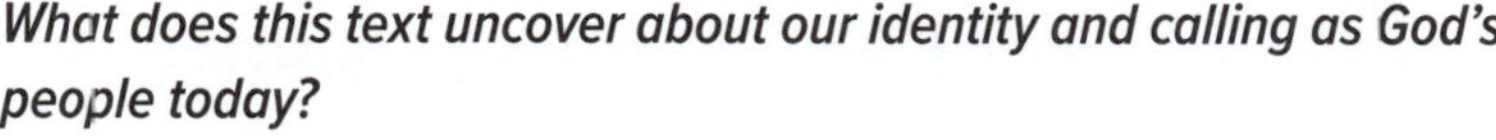

***What does this text uncover about our identity and calling as God's people today?***
Deborah and Jael served God in their various vocations. Deborah the prophetess sits under a tree and helps manage disputes among the people. Jael serves in her husband's tent. God used them as they lived out their daily callings. So, too, we are called to love God and serve our neighbor wherever God has placed us. He will likely not call us to a duty as spectacular as that of these women, but He calls us to serve all the same.

What details about the main characters Deborah and Barak stick out to you? Why?

In what ways does this narrative illustrate how God's methods for accomplishing His work are beyond our plans or understanding?

How can you use your position of authority or influence to love and serve your neighbor today?

### CLEAR THE CONFUSION

**What does the Bible say about women in leadership roles?**

Throughout the Old and New Testaments, God makes it clear that He desires that only men would serve as priests and pastors. God also calls men to leadership in the family, not to domineer but to love and serve those in their charge. God designed men and women to serve in a variety of roles in society, the family, and the church. Deborah was a prophetess, communicating God's truth to those around her. There are other prophetesses throughout the Scriptures, including Miriam and Anna. Deborah understood that ideally she would not lead the men to war, as this was not her role. She begrudgingly did go to war, however, as Barak had too many doubts to do it alone.

How does this song enhance the account of the battle from the previous chapter?

## The Song of Deborah and Barak (5:1–31)

Deborah and Barak sing a song of victory, praising God for raising up the tribes and leaders to fight together. The song also praises Jael for her role. God's people enjoy peace for forty years.

## Midian Oppresses Israel (6:1–10)

God's people do evil in His sight again, and He subjects them to the Midianites for seven years. The Midianites are descendants of Abraham's son through Keturah, the wife Abraham took after Sarah's death (Genesis 25:1–2). The Israelites cry out to God to remember how He had delivered them from Egypt.

Looking at the text, how would you describe Gideon? Would you say he's more shrewd or more scared? Why?

## The Call of Gideon (6:11–27)

The Angel of the Lord appears to Gideon and calls him to deliver God's people. Gideon asks for a sign, which the Angel of the Lord does by consuming a meal in a holy fire. God commands Gideon to destroy his father's idols, and Gideon does so at night out of fear of his neighbors.

## Gideon Destroys the Altar of Baal (6:28–35)

When the people of the town learn their altar has been torn down by Gideon, they call for his death. When Baal fails to punish Gideon for the act, however, the Spirit of the Lord descends on Gideon, and he calls the tribes together to defeat the Midianites and their allies.

## The Sign of the Fleece (6:36–40)

Gideon asks for two signs from God to prove God will save His people. God patiently performs two miraculous signs at Gideon's request.

## Gideon's Three Hundred Men (7:1–18)

### WAYPOINT

***What does this text show us?***

Thirty-two thousand men gather with Gideon, ready to fight. God tells Gideon that is too many men, because when they win, they will be tempted to boast in their own power. God reduces the number to three hundred men, then tells Gideon to secretly surround the enemy camp that night. Gideon formulates an attack plan.

***What does this text reveal about God's plan of salvation?***

God makes it clear that He alone is giving Israel the victory; it is not due to human strength, ambition, or power. God gives victory to Israel because of His faithfulness to His promise. Likewise, He gives victory to us over death through Christ and Christ alone.

***What does this text uncover about our identity and calling as God's people today?***

Because of our sinful human condition, we want to take credit for the good things that happen in our lives. Through Christ, God has defeated the powers of sin, death, and hell for us. Living as God's children, we thank and praise Him for His faithfulness.

What would it be like to be part of Gideon's army? What emotions would you experience? Why?

What parallels do you see between how God worked with Gideon and how God worked through other appointed leaders in the Bible?

What lessons about life as God's people can we learn from the way God interacted with Gideon in this passage?

## Gideon Defeats Midian (7:19–25)

### VISUALIZE

Gideon commanded the three hundred men to surround the camp of the enemy. At Gideon's signal, each of his men broke a pot enclosing a torch and blew a trumpet. God caused the men in the enemy camp to panic, and they fought and killed one another. The remainder of the enemy army fled, and Gideon called out the Israelites of the hill country of Ephraim to join in the enemy rout.

## Gideon Defeats Zebah and Zalmunna (8:1–21)

When the Israelite people of Succoth and Penuel refuse to help Gideon pursue the Midanites, Gideon vows to take vengeance on them. After defeating the remaining Midianite forces and executing the kings Gideon takes revenge on the Israelites who refused him aid.

## Gideon's Ephod (8:22–28)

The people want to make Gideon king, but he refuses. Instead, to keep his control over the people, Gideon commissions an extravagant religious ephod (a kind of garment like the one Israel's high priest wore) that the people worship as a false idol. The land has peace for forty years.

Think of leaders God has placed over you. Which have been a blessing? Why? Which have caused large problems?

## The Death of Gideon (8:29–35)

Gideon has seventy sons from various wives, as well as one notorious son, Abimelech, from a concubine. As soon as Gideon dies, the people turn again to false gods. Instead of delivering Israel into the hands of enemy nations, God delivers them into the ruthless hands of Abimelech.

**CLEAR THE CONFUSION**

**What happened at the end of Gideon's reign?**

After delivering Israel, Gideon quickly became a dictatorial warlord. He made the ephod to retain his position as a spiritual leader (though Israel already had a high priest from Aaron's line). He had a massive family of at least seventy sons through many wives. He named his notorious son *Abimelech*, which means "my father is king."

## Abimelech's Conspiracy (9:1–21)

Abimelech uses money from Baal's temple to hire mercenaries to capture and ritually execute his seventy brothers, the sons of Gideon. The people of Shechem make him king. Jotham, the only one of Gideon's sons who survived the coup, tells a parable foretelling Abimelech's downfall.

## The Downfall of Abimelech (9:22–57)

After three years of Abimelech's rule in central Israel, the people of Shechem rebel against their worthless king. Abimelech goes to punish the people of Shechem and is himself killed. God returns the evil of Abimelech and the people of Shechem who had set up Abimelech as king.

## Tola and Jair (10:1–5)

After relating Abimelech's evils, God raises up two minor judges, Tola and Jair, who judge Israel for a combined forty-five years.

### SET THE SCENE

**Jair, Thirty Donkeys, Thirty Cities, and Polygamy**

Jair kept peace through placing his thirty sons as agents in thirty cities. Though not technically a king, Jair followed the warlord pattern set by Gideon and Abimelech. This shows God's people spiraling away from the ideal governance model God had established when the Israelites settled in the Promised Land.

## Further Disobedience and Oppression (10:6–18)

When Israel turns to worship false gods again, it is oppressed by foreign powers for eighteen years. When they cry out to God, He tells them to cry out to their false gods to save them instead. The people put away their foreign idols, and God becomes impatient over the misery of His people.

## Jephthah Delivers Israel (11:1–28)

### WAYPOINT

***What does this text show us?***
When the Ammonites make war against Israel, Jephthah, the son of a prostitute cast out by his father's other children, is chosen to lead Israel's armies. When the Ammonites claim the Israelites invaded their land, Jephthah shows Israel's proper claim to the lands east of the Jordan. The Ammonites refuse to listen.

***What does this text reveal about God's plan of salvation?***
Jephthah is an outcast, a leader among thugs and mercenaries. But Jephthah knows the narrative of God's plan of salvation, and God uses him as a diplomat to communicate His truth. Throughout the Scriptures, God raises up leaders from all corners of society to do His work.

***What does this text uncover about our identity and calling as God's people today?***
Using discretion and God-given wisdom, we also can acknowledge that God can and does use social outcasts to further His kingdom. We would do well, keeping in line with God's Word, to look past our biases when we look at our neighbor.

What details from this section show that Jephthah is an unusual leader and judge for Israel?

In what ways does this narrative illustrate how God's methods for accomplishing His work are beyond our plans or understanding?

How has God called unexpected people to serve in your congregation? How can you serve using your particular gifts and position?

**How was David similar to Jephthah?**

As we will see in 1 Samuel, David's experience was similar to Jephthah. Both were driven from home—Jephthah by his half brothers, David by King Saul. While in exile, both men found that other outcasts gravitated toward them—outcasts who became great warriors and delivered Israel from their enemies.

## Jephthah's Tragic Vow (11:29–40)

The Spirit of the Lord descends upon Jephthah, who marshals Israel to fight the Ammonites. Before the battle, he makes a rash vow so that God would give him the victory. Jephthah wins, but pays a terrible price for his vow.

CLEAR THE CONFUSION

What vows have you made in your life? Which were rash and which were carefully thought out?

**Why did Jephthah make such a rash vow?**

Jephthah believed to get something great from God, he had to give something valuable in return. He didn't understand that God's gifts are by His grace alone. We can bring nothing, not even human sacrifice, to add to or increase His love for us, because of His complete gift in Jesus.

Though Jephthah may have physically sacrificed his daughter, some commentators suggest she was instead dedicated to serve in the tabernacle at Shiloh (much like what later happened with Samuel). If this is the case, she was given wholly to serve the Lord and was never able to marry.

## Jephthah's Conflict with Ephraim (12:1–7)

Men from the tribe of Ephraim confront Jephthah and threaten to kill the Gileadites for not calling them to participate in the victory over the Ammonites. In self defense, the Gileadites slaughter forty-two thousand Ephraimites. Jephthah dies after judging Israel for six years.

## Ibzan, Elon, and Abdon (12:8–15)

After Jephthah, God raises up three minor judges: Ibzan, Elon, and Abdon, who judge for a total of twenty-five years. During the time these men judged, no conflicts or invasions of foreign powers are recorded.

**CLEAR THE CONFUSION**

**Why do some judges get lots of attention and others very little?**

Certain judges, such as Gideon and Samson, got a lot of attention in the book, while others (often called minor judges) got only a mention. Were the "minor judges" any less faithful or important? No! Based on the judges like Gideon and Samson, it's likely that those who got more mention struggled most with faithfulness. The minor judges did God's work without great drama.

## The Birth of Samson (13:1–25)

When Israel again turns to idolatry, the Angel of the Lord, the preincarnate Christ, appears to the wife of a man named Manoah. He tells her she will bear a child who will follow a specific Nazirite vow. They name their son Samson, and God's Spirit stirs in him.

**SET THE SCENE**

**What were the Nazirite vows?**

Taking the Nazirite vow (*Nazirite* means "dedication") involved not cutting the hair, drinking wine or strong drink, or being close to dead bodies (see Numbers 6:1–20). These vows were often temporary and involved fasting, personal reflection, or piety (see Acts 21:17–26). Samson, however, was consecrated as a Nazirite from birth, since his life was set apart for special service to God.

## Samson's Marriage (14:1–20)

Samson marries a Philistine woman, violating God's command to Israel. At the wedding, he poses a riddle to his thirty Philistine companions. When they threaten Samson's wife, she pressures him and he explains the riddle to her. When she tells the men, Samson's fury stirs.

## Samson Defeats the Philistines (15:1–20)

**WAYPOINT**

***What does this text show us?***

When Samson learns his wife had been given to one of his thirty companions, he burns the Philistine crops. The enraged Philistines kill Samson's wife and her father. Samson takes revenge, then kills one thousand Philistines who come to capture him. He judges Israel for twenty years.

Looking back at the previous sections, trace the series of events that began with Samson desiring marriage to a Philistine woman and ended with Samson killing one thousand men.

What are the parallels between how God used Samson and how Christ conquered sin and death for us?

What can you learn from Samson's example of what to avoid when making decisions in daily life?

***What does this text reveal about God's plan of salvation?***

God faithfully does His work despite human sin and brokenness. Samson was a flagrant sinner, yet many of his actions foreshadowed what Christ would do to deliver God's people one thousand years later.

***What does this text uncover about our identity and calling as God's people today?***

Though God delivers His people through him, Samson's actions are a cautionary tale for us. Samson flaunts God's command not to marry those outside the faith, which sets off the chain reaction of violent events. His other sinful actions caused much pain, harm, destruction, and death to himself and others. Let us learn from Samson to seek to follow God's Word and live with wisdom.

## Samson and Delilah (16:1–22)

After staying with a prostitute in Gaza, Samson loves a woman named Delilah. When bribed by five Philistine kings, she pressures Samson and learns the secret of his strength. He is shaved in his sleep and his strength leaves him. He is bound, blinded, and made to work in a prison mill.

### CLEAR THE CONFUSION

**Why did Samson tell Delilah about his hair?**

Samson appears to have had a sense of entitled invincibility and utter lack of self-control with his passions. The cutting of his hair was likely the last holdout of his commitment to his Nazirite vow. It was not the loss of hair that took Samson's strength but the complete breaking of his vow.

## The Death of Samson (16:23–31)

### VISUALIZE

The lords of the Philistines held a great sacrifice to their false gods for delivering Samson to them. Samson was brought between two pillars to be mocked. He prayed that God would strengthen him once more to die with the Philistines. God granted Samson's prayer. Samson pushed down the temple pillars, killing himself and three thousand Philistine leaders. His family buried his body in his father's tomb.

**PICTURE OF THE SAVIOR**

**Samson**

In one last act of sacrifice, Samson demonstrated a degree of Christ's death well in advance of His world-changing life, death, and resurrection. Shackled, paraded before his enemies, and mocked, Samson prayed fervently to God . In this cry of repentance, God heard Samson and gave him immense strength to collapse the pillars he rested upon. These pillars supported the structure of the entire temple, and thousands of Philistines were killed.

In a similar fashion, Jesus seemed to have been defeated by the powers of the world on the cross, but in reality, His death on the two posts of the cross and resurrection nullified the power of sin and death itself! Samson gave his imperfect life to destroy the enemies of Israel; Jesus gave His perfect life to redeem all mankind and destroy our enemies of sin, death, Satan, and hell.

How does Samson's death help you better appreciate your Savior Jesus' death for you?

# The Dual Epilogue (17:1–21:25)

The final five chapters of Judges are out of sync chronologically from the rest of the book, but they show the continual spiral of God's people away from trusting and serving Him alone. The two brutal ending scenes (epilogues) set the stage for Samuel and King David, who will seek to bring God's people back to true worship of Him.

**SET THE SCENE**

**What are the indicators of a fourteenth-century dating of the epilogues?**

Several sections in the text point to this ending actually happening much earlier in the narrative of the book. In the first epilogue, Micah's Levite is identified as Jonathan, the grandson of Moses (18:30). This, along with the comment that the people of the tribe of Dan were looking for a land to settle, places the date of this epilogue very early in the time of the conquest.

In the second epilogue, the priest who ministered before God during the war against Benjamin is identified as Phinehas, the grandson of Aaron (20:28), who played an important role among God's people before and during the conquest (Numbers 25:7–8; Joshua 22:10–34). These two horrible episodes must have occurred very early in the time of the conquest of the Promised Land.

## Micah and the Levite (17:1–13)

A dishonest Ephraimite named Micah creates idols to worship in the place of the Lord. He hires a Levite, ordained to serve the priests of the true God, to serve as a priest at his shrine.

## Danites Take the Levite and the Idol (18:1–31)

Men from Dan, the tribe that failed to conquer the land allotted to it during the conquest, defeat a group of local Sidonians and take their land. They steal Micah's idols, and convince the Levite, named Jonathan, to serve as priest in their new false shrine.

**CLEAR THE CONFUSION**

**Why didn't the tribe of Dan have land?**

Judges 1:34 shows the Danites were allotted land along the Mediterranean coast but were pushed back by the Amorites. Instead of trusting God to empower them to conquer their land inheritance, they settle for an easier part of the region. This failure to conquer the land God had chosen for them allowed idolatrous nations to remain and live entrenched among the Israelites—which would lead to great temptation and tragedy in the coming centuries.

## A Levite and His Concubine (19:1–21)

In the second epilogue, another Levite retrieves his unfaithful concubine from her father's house. On the return journey they stay in Gibeah, in the tribe of Benjamin. An old man takes them into his house, mirroring the account of the two angels who were taken in by the hospitality of Abraham's nephew Lot in the city of Sodom (see Genesis 19).

How do you think the people of Israel became capable of such vile evil in such a short time? What does that teach you about yourself?

## Gibeah's Crime (19:22–30)

Similar to the Sodom account, a group of worthless Israelites from Gibeah demand that the old man give them the Levite to rape and abuse. The old man refuses, and the Levite gives the men his concubine, whom they abuse until morning, when she dies. The Levite sends a report to the tribes that stirs them to action.

### CLEAR THE CONFUSION

**Why was the Levite so callous?**

It is shocking to think of the Levite carefully dissecting the corpse of his concubine the same way he dissected sacrifices. But he had already shown his true character when he pushed her outside into grave danger to save himself. A worthy man of God would have sacrificed himself to protect her. Then he waited until sunrise to step outside. Even then, his first concern was not her well-being but resuming his journey.

## Israel's War with the Tribe of Benjamin (20:1–48)

### VISUALIZE

The twelve tribes gather at the Levite's summons, and he reports what happened in Gibeah. Outraged, the leaders of Israel follow God's directives in Deuteronomy 13:12–18, demanding Benjamin to turn over the Gibeonites for destruction. Benjamin defies God and the other tribes, refusing to hand them over. A war ensues, with only six hundred men of the tribe of Benjamin remaining.

Instead of being grieved by the evil city in its midst, the tribe of Benjamin went to war to defend it. When have you assisted evil rather than standing up against it?

## Wives Provided for the Tribe of Benjamin (21:1–25)

At the outbreak of the war, the men of Israel vowed not to allow other tribes to ever intermarry with Benjaminite men. Now, with so few Benjaminite men remaining and the women destroyed, the Israelites regret their vow and resort to murder and kidnapping to save the tribe.

### CLEAR THE CONFUSION

**What did the statement "Everyone did what was right in his own eyes" (21:25) mean?**

Instead of letting God's Law inform their minds, they did what was right in their own eyes, as we often do. This attitude compounds one sin upon another.

# RUTH

## Welcome to Ruth

During the period of Judges and the dreadful downward spiral that happened, many faithful Israelites were caught up in the sufferings that resulted from the unfaithfulness of their fellow Israelites. The book of Ruth shows us a group of believers who experience God's faithfulness in the midst of horrible calamities.

Describe a time you were an innocent victim of someone else's poor decision, recklessness, or unfaithfulness.

## Ruth at a Glance

- **Start:** The book of Ruth begins in the time of the judges with a family forced to leave Bethlehem because of famine.
- **End:** Ruth ends with one member of that family holding her grandchild whose line leads to David.
- **Theme:** Ruth shows God's faithfulness to a single family during a time of faithlessness and suffering.
- **Author and Date:** The author is unknown but is likely someone connected to David's kingship. It was written around 1000 BC.
- **Places Visited:** Bethlehem in Judah, Moab
- **Journey Time:** The four chapters of Ruth can be read in about fifteen minutes.
- **Outline:**
  - The Dilemma (1:1–22)
  - The Hope (2:1–23)
  - The Risk (3:1–18)
  - The Solution (4:1–22)

What are some ways God has shown His faithfulness to you and your family?

## Five Top Sights and Spectacles of Ruth

**Tragedy in Moab (1:1–5)** Feel Naomi's pain when her husband and two sons die in Moab.

**Naomi's Return (1:6–22)** Watch Naomi try to convince her daughters-in-law to remain as she returns in sorrow to Bethlehem.

**Ruth in Bethlehem (2:1–23)** Follow Ruth as she gathers leftover crops in the fields of Boaz and is accepted by him.

**Naomi and Ruth Risk Everything (3:1–18)** Hear Naomi's risky plan to solve their dilemma, and see Ruth's challenge to Boaz.

**Boaz's Resolve (4:1–17)** Watch noble Boaz step up to rescue Naomi and Ruth from their perilous situation.

## Seeing Jesus in Ruth

Naomi and Ruth live as widows in Bethlehem. A kinsman named Boaz redeems Ruth to be his wife and provides for Naomi as a son. In Boaz, we see a reflection of Jesus, who went to the cross to redeem us from the perils of our sins and to take His church as His Bride forever.

## The Dilemma (1:1–22)

An Israelite father, mother, and two sons sojourn in Moab. When the father and both sons die in Moab, the widowed mother, Naomi, returns to Israel. Her daughter-in-law Ruth joins her to live as a widow in Israel.

What are some hardships you have suffered that have changed your life forever?

### Naomi Widowed (1:1–5)

During the time of the judges, famine drives this family of four from Bethlehem to Moab. Over the course of ten years, the father, Elimelech, dies; the two sons, Mahlon and Chilion, marry Moabite women and then both die, leaving Naomi with only her two daughters-in-law.

**CLEAR THE CONFUSION**

**Why did Elimelech and Naomi sojourn in Moab?**

One of Israel's judges, Ehud, defeated Moab (Judges 3:12–30) and Israel occupied some of its territory. It is likely Elimelech and Naomi sojourned in this occupied part of Moab to avoid places where foreign gods were worshiped.

### Ruth's Loyalty to Naomi (1:6–18)

When Naomi heard the famine had lifted she decided to return to Bethlehem. Not wanting her daughters-in-law to be condemned to a life of poverty, she urged them to return to their homes and their Moabite gods. Orpah renounced her faith in Israel's God and returned to the gods of Moab. Ruth pledged to stay with her mother-in-law and serve the God of Israel.

### Naomi and Ruth Return (1:19–22)

Naomi and Ruth return to Bethlehem. When approached by the women in town, Naomi tells them to call her Mara on account of her bitterness and shame.

What do you think of Naomi complaining about how the Almighty has dealt bitterly with her? When have you struggled through similar feelings about God?

## The Hope (2:1–23)

When Ruth gleans leftover food in the fields of a good man named Boaz, he befriends her, giving Naomi hope that Boaz may be willing to redeem her late husband's inheritance and marry Ruth.

**How did widows, orphans, and foreigners survive in Israel?**

Widows, orphans, and foreigners went out into fields and orchards to gather what was left behind after the harvest. God designed Israel to be a nation that reflected His care and concern for struggling people. He even commanded farmers to intentionally leave the edges of their fields unharvested for the needy among Israel (see Leviticus 23:22). Boaz's kind treatment of Ruth shows how much he loved the Lord his God and lived as God directed.

Describe an unexpected act of kindness someone once did for you. What impact did that have on your relationship with that person?

### Ruth Meets Boaz (2:1–23)

Ruth goes into a stranger's field to glean. God guides her to the field of Boaz, a prominent man who is a close relative of Elimelech. Boaz notices her and directs his reapers to leave choice pickings of grain behind and to let her drink the water they have drawn.

## The Risk (3:1–18)

Ruth risks public rejection and worse when Naomi instructs her to dress as a bride and spend the night next to Boaz as he sleeps on the threshing floor.

Describe the great risk Ruth took, not knowing if Boaz would accept or reject her. What is a risk you have taken by stepping out in faith, trusting God to guide you?

### Ruth and Boaz at the Threshing Floor (3:1–18)

Seeing that Boaz would be a wonderful husband for Ruth, Naomi sends her, dressed as a bride, to the threshing floor where Boaz is feasting after a long day of harvest. Boaz promises to redeem and marry her in the morning if a nearer relative will not.

**CLEAR THE CONFUSION**

**What did it mean to "redeem" in the Old Testament?**

Israelites were not permitted to sell the land passed down from ancestors. Instead they sold the right to grow and harvest crops on that land. The land was automatically restored every fifty years in the year of jubilee. When Elimelech and Naomi left Bethlehem years before, they had sold the rights to the crops grown on his ancestral property. This is why Ruth had to glean in Boaz's field instead of reaping directly in her late father-in-law Elimelech's field.

Boaz agreed not only to redeem the rights to the harvest so Ruth and Naomi could grow their own food but also to marry Ruth and raise up offspring for Elimelech to keep the family inheritance intact. Boaz himself would not take ownership of that property; it would pass to his child (with Ruth), who would become the heir to Elimelech's inheritance.

## The Solution (4:1–22)

The next morning, Boaz redeems Ruth when the nearer kinsman is unable to. Ruth and Boaz marry and have a son, who continues the line leading to King David and ultimately to the Savior, Jesus Christ.

## Boaz Redeems Ruth (4:1–12)

### WAYPOINT

***What does this text show us?***
Boaz meets with the closer relative who is prepared to fulfil his obligation, until he learns Ruth needs a husband. The unnamed relative then refuses, and Boaz takes the right of redemption. He agrees to marry Ruth and produce an heir for Naomi's family to keep the property.

***What does this text reveal about God's plan of salvation?***
Boaz was an ancestor of the promised Christ. He befriended a Gentile woman, taking her as his bride and redeeming her by his own wealth. Boaz gives us a glimpse into Jesus Christ, our Savior, who takes us as His own Bride and redeems us with His holy, precious blood and His innocent suffering and death.

***What does this text uncover about our identity and calling as God's people today?***
Like Ruth, we have received God's abundant mercy and grace, been forgiven all our sins, and been made God's own Bride. Like her, we show our love and gratitude to our Savior through lives of loving service.

Boaz shows his noble character by promptly following up on his promise. Describe a promise you made and promptly kept. What impact did it have on the person to whom you made the promise?

How does the picture of bride and groom help you better understand the relationship between God and His people?

What parts of Ruth's story remind you of God's grace in your life?

## Ruth and Boaz Marry (4:13–17)

### VISUALIZE

Boaz married Ruth and had a son with her. They named him Obed, and the women of Bethlehem praised the Lord for His loving kindness to Naomi and her family. Naomi was overjoyed and became a nurse to the baby.

## The Genealogy of David (4:18–22)

The line from Boaz and Ruth is traced down to King David, whose story will be picked up in our next book, 1 Samuel.

# 1 SAMUEL

## Welcome to 1 Samuel

1 Samuel describes how Israel demands a king. The people reject not merely the rule of judges but more importantly God's rule over them through His covenant. God remains faithful and furthers His promise of a Savior to crush the serpent's head (see Genesis 3:15).

What narratives are you familiar with from 1 Samuel? What are some specific things you would like to learn more about?

## 1 Samuel at a Glance

- **Start:** The book begins with the birth of the prophet Samuel.
- **End:** The book ends with the death of King Saul, Israel's first king.
- **Theme:** 1 Samuel explores the effects of faithful and unfaithful leadership upon God's people.
- **Author and Date:** The author of 1 Samuel is unknown. Both 1 and 2 Samuel were written as one book around 970 BC.
- **Places Visited:** Region of Benjamin, Ephraim, Philistia, and Judah
- **Journey Time:** The thirty-one chapters of 1 Samuel can be read in about two hours.
- **Outline:**
  - The Birth and Calling of Samuel (1:1–3:21)
  - The Ark and the Lord's Presence (4:1–7:2)
  - Changing Leadership (7:3–12:25)
  - King Saul's Crisis (13:1–15:35)
  - Saul and David (16:1–31:13)

## Five Top Sights and Spectacles of 1 Samuel

**The Lord Calls Samuel (3:1–21)** Listen as the Lord speaks Samuel's name in the night, calling him into the service of God.

**David Anointed King (16:1–13)** Follow along as Samuel rejects each of Jesse's sons until the youngest, David, is chosen as the future king.

**David and Goliath (17:1–58)** Watch in amazement as a brave young shepherd comes forward to battle a gigantic enemy warrior.

**Jonathan Warns David (20:1–42)** Experience the incredible friendship between Jonathan and David.

**David Spares Saul Again (26:1–25)** Stand in the midst of Saul's war camp as David holds Saul's life in his hands.

## Seeing Jesus in 1 Samuel

There are striking parallels between David's life and Jesus' life. Both were anointed (David by Samuel, Jesus by John the Baptist); persecuted and pursued by jealous people who sought their lives; and exalted to the throne (David in Jerusalem, Jesus at the Father's right hand in heaven).

## The Birth and Calling of Samuel (1:1–3:21)

When childless Hannah prays in great grief, God grants her a son, Samuel, whom she dedicates for full-time service to the Lord. We learn the wickedness of the sons of the high priest Eli. God calls young Samuel and announces His judgment on Eli's family.

### The Birth of Samuel (1:1–20)

Elkanah, a man from Ephraim, has two wives. Peninnah, who has many children, endlessly harasses Hannah, who has none. During their annual pilgrimage to Shiloh, Hannah tells Eli the high priest of her desire for a child. He blesses Hannah, and God opens her womb.

### Samuel Given to the LORD (1:21–28)

***What does this text show us?***
When Samuel has been weaned—probably at around three years old—Hannah takes him to the tabernacle to offer sacrifices to God. In keeping with her promise, Hannah gives Samuel to the Lord for the duration of his life.

How do you think Samuel was affected by growing up in the tabernacle?

***What does this text reveal about God's plan of salvation?***
When Hannah brings young Samuel to Eli, she dedicates her son to the Lord for His work. At just the right time, God will send His own Son, to give His life and His very self as the ultimate sacrifice for sin.

***What does this text uncover about our identity and calling as God's people today?***
Samuel was dedicated to the service of the Lord for his lifetime. While God might not be calling us to full-time service to Him, we have opportunities to serve Him and others in the world through our gifts and talents.

Hannah offers the sacrifices for her son. How has Christ offered the sacrifice for us?

How can you give thanks to those who have chosen to serve the Lord in a full-time capacity?

## Hannah's Prayer (2:1–11)

Hannah offers a prayer thanking God for His miraculous work in her life. The prayer offers a number of contrasts between the world's wisdom and God's wisdom. Hannah repeatedly praises the Lord for His mercy and grace displayed in her life.

**LINK BETWEEN THE TESTAMENTS**

**Hannah's Prayer → Mary's Prayer (1 Samuel 2:1–10 → Luke 1:46–55)**

In their prayers, both Hannah and Mary praise God for His faithfulness and marvel at His way of exalting humble believers and humbling the proud.

## Eli's Worthless Sons (2:12–21)

Eli the high priest has two sons, Hophni and Phinehas, who are called "worthless men." They do not know the Lord and abuse the offerings brought to them. Young Samuel, by contrast, serves the Lord faithfully.

## Eli Rebukes His Sons (2:22–26)

Eli rebukes his sons for abusing God's sacrifices and committing sexual sins with the women who work at the entrance to the tent of meeting. Having no fear of God, the sons ignore their father's direction and continue in their sinful ways.

## The LORD Rejects Eli's Household (2:27–36)

An unnamed prophet warns Eli that God has rejected him and his sons. As high priest, Eli had the authority to stop his sons but allowed them to profane God's sacrifices. He learns both sons will fall by the sword on the same day. In their place, God will raise up faithful ministers.

## The LORD Calls Samuel (3:1–21)

### WAYPOINT

Read through 1 Samuel 3 again. What information in this chapter surprises you?

***What does this text show us?***

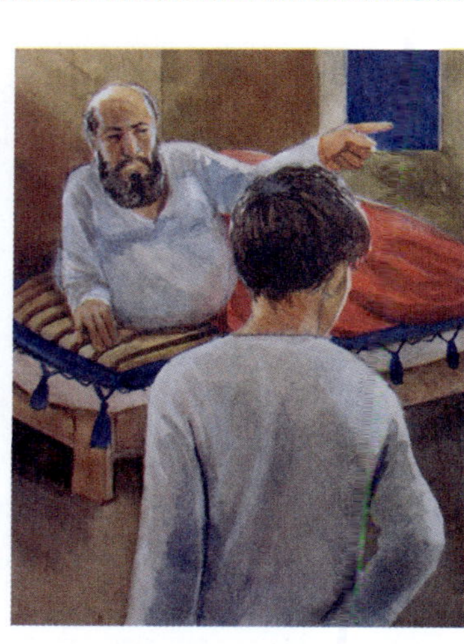

While sleeping in the tabernacle, Samuel hears a voice calling to him which he thinks is Eli. When the voice calls him two more times, Eli instructs him how to answer the one truly calling him: God. When the Lord calls Samuel a fourth time, Samuel quickly responds. The Lord reveals the dire fate of Eli and his family.

God gives Samuel a glimpse of His plan of salvation as He appears and calls Samuel into full-time service. What question might you have about God's plan?

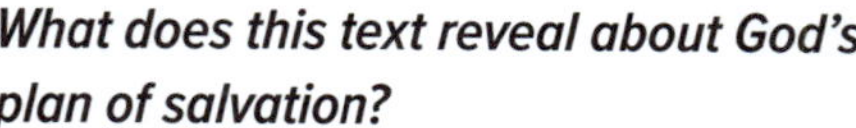

***What does this text reveal about God's plan of salvation?***

God appears before Samuel and calls him to serve Him as prophet, priest, and judge. One day, God's Son will come in human form as the baby born to Mary. Jesus will serve as our Prophet, Priest, and King. Through Him, we receive forgiveness, life, and salvation.

What has God called you to do for Him in service toward others?

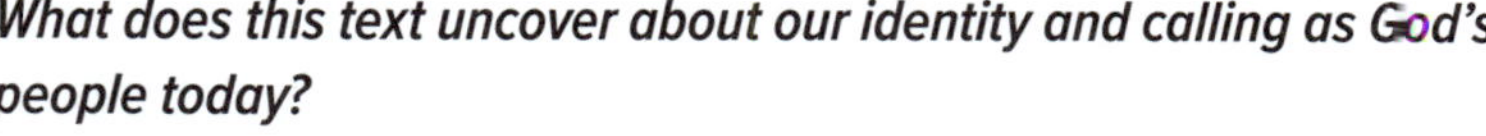

***What does this text uncover about our identity and calling as God's people today?***

God calls us to be His people through the Word and Sacraments. But God calls some to serve Him in specific ministry roles within the church, much as He called Samuel as prophet and priest. But all of us can serve God as we use the gifts and talents He gives us to serve one another.

### PICTURE OF THE SAVIOR

**Samuel**

The book of 1 Samuel tells us the Word of God was rarely spoken to leaders in Israel in those days, but the Lord called Samuel to serve as prophet, priest, and judge of Israel.

Jesus came as a babe at Bethlehem, born of Mary by the power of the Holy Spirit. Jesus replaced the lineage of earthly prophets and priests as our

one eternal Prophet, Priest, and King. The sacrifice He made is a once-for-all sacrifice. Christ paid the price for our sins through His death and resurrection.

# The Ark and the Lord's Presence (4:1–7:2)

The Philistines defeat Israel in battle and capture the ark of the covenant. When God lays a heavy hand on the Philistines, they return the ark to Israel.

## The Philistines Capture the Ark (4:1–11)

After suffering great losses in battle against the Philistines, Israel sends to Shiloh for the ark of the covenant—not because they have repented and trust in God but because they see it as a good luck charm. The Philistines rally their troops and win a decisive battle.

How could the capture of the ark have been disastrous for God's reputation? How is God able to protect His saving reputation in Jesus when sinful Christian leaders act in shameful and disgraceful ways?

## The Death of Eli (4:12–22)

Eli learns both his sons have died in battle, but when he hears the Philistines have captured the ark, he falls and dies. The Philistines destroy much of Shiloh, the place where the tabernacle had been set up and the Israelites had gathered for generations for the annual festivals.

## The Philistines and the Ark (5:1–12)

The Philistines place the ark before the idol of Dagon in Ashdod. But the next morning, they find Dagon lying on his face before the ark. The next day he is back on the floor with his head and hands cut off. When the ark was moved to Gath the people broke out with tumors, which happened again when the ark was moved to Ekron. The Philistines decided to return the ark to Israel.

### The Ark Returned to Israel (6:1–7:2)

The return of the ark brought great joy to the Israelites, but that joy was quickly changed to fear when they failed to honor God and treat the ark as holy. How might this event guide our attitude toward the Lord's Supper?

**VISUALIZE**

When the Philistines prepare to return the ark, they add a chest with gold tumors and mice in an attempt to appease Israel's mighty God. The ark is loaded on a cart pulled by milk cows and sent away to the Israelites. In Beth-shemesh some Israelites look into the ark and are struck down.

**PICTURE OF THE SAVIOR**

**The Ark Returns**

Christ's coming in the New Testament ushered in a new perspective concerning God's presence with His people and the need for sin offerings. No longer was God's presence confined to the ark; rather, He is Immanuel: "God with us" (Matthew 1:23). In Christ, the need for sin offerings was met once for all time through His death and resurrection.

## Changing Leadership (7:3–12:25)

Samuel serves as Israel's prophet, priest, and final judge. When he grows old, Israel demands a king. God chooses Saul of the tribe of Benjamin to be Israel's first king.

### Samuel Judges Israel (7:3–17)

Once again, God protects His people in an amazing way. How does God protect us today?

Twenty years after the return of the ark, Samuel calls all the people to gather at Mizpah to fast and repent. When the Philistines attack Israel the people call out to God in fear, and Samuel prepares a burnt offering. The Lord thunders, sending the Philistines into confusion.

## Israel Demands a King (8:1–9)

When Samuel grows old, he appoints his two sons as judges in Beersheba. Sadly, his sons seek their own gain, as Eli's sons had done. Seeing that Samuel's sons will not become faithful judges, the leaders of the Israelites ask him to appoint a king to rule over them.

Most of us don't have a king ruling over our nation. How could the leader of a nation influence the faith life of that nation either negatively or positively?

### CLEAR THE CONFUSION

**Why did Israel want a king?**

Israel's desire to move away from the leadership of the judges to a monarchy indicated a desire by many to avoid the distinct character God wanted their lives to have as His people. God reminded Samuel that this request was not a rejection of Samuel as their judge but a rejection of God Himself.

## Samuel's Warning Against Kings (8:10–18)

Samuel returns to the people with dire warnings against their desire for a king. Despite warnings concerning everything from the king taking their children as servants to the burden of additional taxation, the people persist in their desire for a king to rule over them.

## The LORD Grants Israel's Request (8:19–22)

Samuel brings the words of the people and their desire for a king before the Lord. Finally, the Lord tells Samuel He will grant the people's request for an earthly king to rule over them.

## Saul Chosen to Be King (9:1–27)

Saul, from the tribe of Benjamin goes searching for his father's missing donkeys. Learning that Samuel is nearby, Saul sets off to consult him. Samuel takes Saul to the high place and treats him as an honored guest. The next morning, Samuel reveals God's plan to Saul.

### CLEAR THE CONFUSION

**What was striking about God's choice of Saul from the tribe of Benjamin?**

In Judges 21, Saul's tribe of Benjamin had been reduced to six hundred men and the wives they had been given. God chose Israel's first king from this humiliated tribe. Notice Saul's surprise as he asked Samuel, "Am I not a Benjaminite, from the least of the tribes of Israel?" (1 Samuel 9:21).

## Saul Anointed King (10:1–16)

Reread this section of Scripture. How are the details in this section both amazing and important?

God sent His only Son, the Anointed One, as the Savior. How does knowing Jesus is God's Anointed One reassure you concerning your salvation?

How has God set you apart to serve Him and others?

***What does this text show us?***

Samuel anoints Saul's head with a flask of oil and reveals God's plan for Saul to rule over the Israelites, protect them from their enemies, and serve as their king. God changes Saul's attitude, which others notice as Saul begins to take on his role as the king of Israel.

***What does this text reveal about God's plan of salvation?***

Samuel anoints Saul as king, and the Spirit of the Lord enters him and brings about great changes in Saul as he begins to prophesy. Similarly, when John the Baptist will baptize Jesus, God the Father will anoint Him with the Holy Spirit.

***What does this text uncover about our identity and calling as God's people today?***

In Holy Baptism, God anointed us as His own children and filled us with the Holy Spirit. As we read, study, and learn from the Word, God guides us in our daily lives to serve Him as royal priests.

## Saul Proclaimed King (10:17–27)

Samuel gathers all Israel together at Mizpah. He reminds them how God brought them out of Egypt, but in their stubbornness, they are now turning aside to have a king. When Samuel tries to present Saul, he is hiding in the baggage. While most welcome Saul, some wonder how this man could possibly be king.

## Saul Defeats the Ammonites (11:1–11)

The Ammonites besiege an Israelite city east of the Jordan River. The Ammonites' condition for peace is gouging out the Israelites' right eyes. When word comes to Saul's town, the people weep in hopelessness. But the Spirit fills Saul with holy wrath.

**SET THE SCENE**

**When would Jabesh-gilead return Saul's favor?**

When Saul died in battle against the Philistines, the valiant men of Jabesh traveled deep within Philistia to recover his body and the bodies of his sons. They burned them so the Philistines could no longer desecrate their remains and buried their bones beneath a tamarisk tree in Jabesh (1 Samuel 31:11–13).

### The Kingdom Is Renewed (11:12–15)

Following the victory at Jabesh-gilead, some want to execute those who had spoken against Saul. Saul prevents this action. Samuel leads the people to Gilgal to renew their commitment to God and the kingdom.

### Samuel's Farewell Address (12:1–25)

Samuel addresses the people at Gilgal. After reminding them of all God has done for them, he warns them against trusting in their king or in false gods. After calling on God to send a storm, Samuel reminds the people to repent and serve God in order to avoid His divine wrath.

Samuel gives his farewell address, but he's not going away any time soon. Why do you suppose this account appears at this point in 1 Samuel?

## King Saul's Crisis (13:1–15:35)

Though anointed with the Holy Spirit, King Saul seeks his own will instead of God's will and is rejected as Israel's king.

**CLEAR THE CONFUSION**

**Why are there numbers missing in the Hebrew text of 1 Samuel 13:1?**

In the Hebrew and its Greek translation (called the Septuagint), Saul's age when he became king and the length of his reign are missing from 1 Samuel 13:1. With the tragic course that Saul's kingship took, it is as if God has erased details of this wicked king's reign.

### Saul Fights the Philistines (13:1–7)

Saul divides his warriors into two groups; one goes with him, the other with his son, Jonathan. Jonathan attacks a garrison of Philistines. The Philistines muster a huge army. In fear, the Israelites hide among the caves and rocks, while others cross the Jordan to the land of Gilead.

## Saul's Unlawful Sacrifice (13:8–23)

Saul's impatience gets the best of him as he unlawfully offers the sacrifice. How can your impatience get the best of you?

### VISUALIZE

Saul waits seven days as Samuel directed, watching as his army scatters and dwindles away to nothing. Instead of waiting for Samuel to come and offer the burnt offering, Saul goes ahead and offers it himself. Samuel arrives as soon as he finishes and warns Saul his reign will not last.

### CLEAR THE CONFUSION

**Why did Samuel chastise Saul when Samuel showed up so late?**

Samuel delayed to test Saul's faith. Did he trust God's promises even if his army dwindled down to nothing and he and Jonathan were all that was left? Saul lost faith in God's help and burned the offering to rally his troops.

## Jonathan Defeats the Philistines (14:1–23)

### VISUALIZE

In strong faith, Jonathan sets out with his armor bearer and kills about twenty Philistine soldiers. Panic sets in among the enemy soldiers, who turn their swords against one another. Through Jonathan's faith, God gives the Israelites victory over the Philistines. Saul just needed to trust God like Jonathan.

## Saul's Rash Vow (14:24–46)

As Saul and his men pursue the fleeing Philistines, he foolishly vows that none of his troops will eat until the sun sets. Unaware of his father's declaration, Jonathan eats some wild honey. When Saul seeks the Lord's direction, he gets no answer because his sacred vow has been broken.

Saul foolishly declares that none of his troops should eat while fighting the Philistines. Do you ever make vows that you later regret? How do you make things right again?

**CLEAR THE CONFUSION**

**What were the Urim and Thummim?**

On Mount Sinai, the Lord directed Moses to make a breastpiece of judgment for the high priest to wear (Exodus 28:30). The Urim and Thummim were two sacred lots placed in this breastpiece. Two options were put forth, and, using the Urim and Thummim, God indicated which of the two options He chose.

## Saul Fights Israel's Enemies (14:47–52)

Saul battles against enemies on every side, including Moab, the Ammonites, the Philistines, Edom, and others. Clearly, Israel has many powerful enemies at this time, as in the days of the judges.

## The LORD Rejects Saul (15:1–35)

**WAYPOINT**

***What does this text show us?***
Through Samuel, God directs Saul to strike Amalek and completely destroy it (see Exodus 17:14). Saul's massive army quickly defeats Amalek, but Saul spares the king and the best of the livestock. Samuel announces that God will tear the kingdom away from Saul and then executes King Agag himself.

***What does this text reveal about God's plan of salvation?***
Through His Word, God calls us to sincerely repent and trust in His gift of salvation, found only through His Son, Jesus Christ. In Christ, we receive forgiveness, life, and salvation for all our doubts and disobedience.

***What does this text uncover about our identity and calling as God's people today?***
Like Saul, we fail to completely follow God's direction. We depend solely on His grace and mercy shown in the person of His own Son, Jesus Christ. In Him, we receive forgiveness for our disobedience and lack of trust. Empowered by the Spirit, through Word and Sacrament, we can serve God and one another.

Review God's directions to Saul concerning Amalek. How does Saul ignore God's direction? What is the consequence of that choice?

After being confronted concerning his sin, Saul finally confesses his wrongs, but his repentance does not last long. Why is it important that we be reminded of our sins and truly repent of them?

How does God empower us to seek His mercy and forgiveness?

 CLEAR THE CONFUSION

**Why did God demand the extermination of the Amalekites?**

The Amalekites descended from Amalek, Esau's son. They attacked Israel between the Red Sea and Mount Sinai (Exodus 17:8–16). On account of this merciless attack, God commanded Moses, "Write this as a memorial in a book and recite it in the ears of Joshua, that I will utterly blot out the memory of Amalek from under heaven" (Exodus 17:14).

# Saul and David (16:1–31:13)

God sends Samuel to anoint David of Bethlehem as king to replace Saul. David comes into Saul's service and is very successful. Saul grows jealous and seeks David's life. After David spares his life twice, Saul is killed in battle against the Philistines.

## David Anointed King (16:1–13)

 VISUALIZE

God told Samuel to stop grieving Saul's rejection and go to Bethlehem to anoint the next king of Israel. When God rejected each of Jesse's older sons, Jesse sent for his youngest son, David. When David appeared, God revealed that this was the man He had chosen to lead Israel. Samuel anointed David before his siblings and father as witnesses.

Why do you think David was important to Israel?

 PICTURE OF THE SAVIOR

**David**

David shared many traits with his greater descendant, Jesus:

1. David and Jesus are both from Bethlehem; in fact, Jesus is a direct descendant of David through His mother.

2. David was secretly anointed as king; in the same way, Jesus' birth came about quietly without any public fanfare.
3. David sought the heart of the Lord his God; in the same way, we see in Jesus' prayers how He constantly sought His Father's will.
4. David would be betrayed by a trusted counselor and his own son; Jesus was betrayed by one of His chosen disciples.

## David in Saul's Service (16:14–23)

Saul is troubled by a harmful spirit. His servants recommend finding a skilled lyre player to help him relax. Since David is a skilled musician, Saul sends for him. David plays his lyre whenever the harmful spirit afflicts Saul. Saul loves David and makes him his trusted armor-bearer.

### CLEAR THE CONFUSION

**Why did the Spirit of the Lord leave Saul?**

The Holy Spirit left Saul because of his disobedience. In the Spirit's absence, Saul became afflicted by a harmful, fallen spirit. God allowed the fallen angel to afflict Saul to bring him to repentance so he might find God's mercy and grace. However, Saul only turned further away from his loving God.

## David and Goliath (17:1–58)

### WAYPOINT

***What does this text show us?***
A Philistine champion named Goliath challenges Israel to choose one man to fight him man on man. Though King Saul offers great gifts to the man who will face the giant, all of his troops are too terrified. When David hears Goliath's blasphemous challenge, the Spirit stirs him to accept.

***What does this text reveal about God's plan of salvation?***
God sent David, a teenager from Bethlehem, to defeat the fearsome giant Goliath. One day God would send His own Son, born in Bethlehem, to defeat our "giant" enemies: sin, death, hell, and Satan. David took down Goliath with his sling and a stone. Jesus defeated our enemies with a cross.

How do you handle conflict? How do you react when you face seemingly impossible challenges?

What connections do you see between the account of David defeating Goliath and Jesus' victory over sin, death, and the devil?

What kinds of "giants" are you facing right now?

***What does this text uncover about our identity and calling as God's people today?***
As God's redeemed people, we serve as His witnesses in our world. We must share our beliefs and values despite the world's objections. When our beliefs conflict with "giants" or popular opinions, the Holy Spirit strengthens us to remain faithful through God's Word and Sacraments.

### CLEAR THE CONFUSION

**How tall was Goliath?**

The Bible gives Goliath's height in cubits and spans. A cubit is the distance from your elbow to your fingertip. A span is the width of your hand. The text of the ESV Bible reports Goliath as "six cubits and a span" (17:4), which could be over nine feet tall. With the Holy Spirit empowering him, David had no fear.

Take a moment to review these verses. What symbols of friendship do you share with your friends?

## David and Jonathan's Friendship (18:1–5)

David and Saul's son Jonathan become inseparable friends after David defeats Goliath. Both are men of great faith in God. In wonderful humility, Jonathan forges a covenant, surrendering his right to Saul's throne.

### PICTURE OF THE SAVIOR

**Ultimate Friendship**

In 1 Samuel 18:1, we read that Jonathan loved David "as his own soul." Later in 1 Samuel, we learn Jonathan put his relationship with his own father at risk in order to rescue David from Saul's jealousy and suspicious threats. In Christ, we have the ultimate friend who laid down His life to save us.

## Saul's Jealousy of David (18:6–16)

God gives David success in everything he does. Remembering Samuel's prediction that God would take the kingdom from him, Saul attempts to pin David to the wall with his spear.

How does Saul's plotting and planning go wrong?

## David Marries Michal (18:17–30)

When Saul learns his younger daughter Michal loves David, he offers her to David if he will bring him the foreskins of one hundred Philistines. David and his men slaughter two hundred Philistines and send twice the bride price to Saul. Saul gives Michal to David but fears him even more.

## Saul Tries to Kill David (19:1–24)

When Saul tells Jonathan he should kill David, Jonathan defends David. But after David has further success against the Philistines, Saul tries to kill David again. He sends soldiers to David's house to kill him in his bed. David flees and seeks Samuel's protection in Naioth.

## Jonathan Warns David (20:1–42)

David asks Jonathan to determine why King Saul hates him so much. When Jonathan defends his friend, Saul hurls his spear at his own son. Indignant at his father's shameful treatment of David, Jonathan sends David into hiding.

Sometimes we say people risk everything for a friend. How is this true for David and Jonathan?

## David and the Holy Bread (21:1–9)

While fleeing from Saul, David receives holy bread from the high priest Ahimelech in the city of Nob. Since he fled without a weapon, David takes the sword of Goliath, which was stored at the tabernacle as a relic honoring God for giving Israel victory over its enemy.

## David Flees to Gath (21:10–15)

David faces such danger in Israel he flees to the Philistine city of Gath. When the servants of King Achish recognize David and his military success leading Israel against their troops, David pretends to be insane. King Achish drives David out.

## David at the Cave of Adullam (22:1–5)

David hides in the cave at Adullam. There he gathers his family and four hundred outcast men gather around him and become his army. David asks the king of Moab to give shelter to his parents, while he flees to a forest in Judah for refuge.

### CLEAR THE CONFUSION

**Why would David send his parents to the king of Moab?**

In the book of Ruth, we saw David's ancestors sojourn in Moab when a famine struck Bethlehem. Naomi brought her daughter-in-law Ruth back to Bethlehem, where Ruth married David's ancestor Boaz. Ruth's connection to Moab was likely why David asked the king of Moab to take care of his parents.

## Saul Kills the Priests at Nob (22:6–23)

An Edomite servant, Doeg, tells Saul that David received help from Ahimelech, the high priest. Saul orders Ahimelech and the other priests to be executed. When Saul's servants refuse, Doeg viciously kills eighty-five priests with their families. Only one priest escapes to warn David.

## David Saves the City of Keilah (23:1–14)

After the Philistines attack the Israelite city of Keilah, God helps David and his army rescue Keilah and drive out the Philistines. When God reveals the men of Keilah will betray their rescuer and surrender him to Saul, David and his troops leave the city before Saul can arrive.

## Saul Pursues David (23:15–29)

Jonathan meets David in Ziph and strengthens his faith, reminding David that God has chosen him as king. The people of Ziph betray David, revealing his location to Saul, who leads the whole Israelite army against David and his men.

## David Spares Saul's Life (24:1–22)

How does David demonstrate his respect for Saul, the king God anointed?

Why does it seem impossible that David refrained from harming Saul? What probably would have happened if the roles were reversed?

When might you face a challenge to respect and honor one of God's chosen ones?

***What does this text show us?***

Saul takes three thousand troops into the wilderness to pursue David. He relieves himself in a cave, not knowing David and his men are hiding in that very cave. Though David's soldiers encourage him to kill Saul, David rebukes them and cuts the corner from Saul's robe instead.

***What does this text reveal about God's plan of salvation?***

While Saul was certainly flawed, God rescued His chosen people through Saul's successful military campaigns. This shows God's faithfulness despite our unfaithfulness. In this way Saul imperfectly prefigured Christ's faithful victory over sin and death.

***What does this text uncover about our identity and calling as God's people today?***

God calls us His children through our Baptism; He gives us His Son, Jesus, as the Anointed Savior. As we live our lives today, we honor Him with our actions, especially when we honor and obey the government officials He places over us (unless they demand we disobey God).

## The Death of Samuel (25:1a)

Israel's great respect for Samuel is evidenced by the nationwide mourning among the people. As Samuel was the only man of God that Saul listened to, Saul now has no godly counselors left. Samuel is laid to rest at Ramah, which served as the base for his entire ministry.

## David and Abigail (25:1b–44)

David guards the herds of a wealthy man named Nabal. At harvesttime, David sends young men to Nabal to request food and water. Nabal arrogantly refuses. David prepares his men to slay Nabal and all his men. Nabal's wife, Abigail, hears and convinces David not to attack.

### CLEAR THE CONFUSION

**Why did David take Abigail as his wife? Wasn't he already married to Saul's daughter Michal?**

Actually, by this time, David had three wives: Michal, Abigail, and Ahinoam of Jezreel. David continued to add wives and concubines in the years to come, causing great strife and turmoil in his family, as we will see in the second book of Samuel.

## David Spares Saul Again (26:1–25)

### VISUALIZE

The people of Ziph betrayed David to Saul At night, Saul and his three thousand chosen men set up camp in the wilderness and fell under a deep sleep from the Lord.

David and his nephew Abishai went into Saul's camp and found Saul asleep next to his commander, Abner. Abishai offered to spear Saul to the ground with one thrust, but instead, David took Saul's spear and jar of water and sneaked away. Once safely out of the camp, David called to Abner and showed him the spear and jar, thus revealing the poor job he had done protecting King Saul.

Once again David has a chance to kill Saul but refuses. In what ways is this account even more dramatic than the previous account?

## David Flees to the Philistines (27:1–12)

David and his six hundred men flee to Gath of the Philistines. King Achish welcomes David, and gives him the city of Ziklag on the border between Israel and Philistia. From there, David and his men make raids on surrounding territories to help the people of Judah.

### CLEAR THE CONFUSION

**Why did the Philistine king Achish welcome and trust David?**

Back in chapter 21, David had just fled Saul for the first time, and the Philistines were unaware of Saul's hatred of David. But by this time, they knew of Saul's efforts to kill David and believed David hated Saul and Israel.

In reality, David misled Achish. When he raided the surrounding territories, Achish assumed he was attacking Israelite cities in retaliation against Saul and making himself a permanent enemy of Israel. But David was raiding Israel's enemies and leaving no survivors to keep Achish from learning the truth.

Saul's behavior has sunk to a new low. How does Saul's attempt to gain information go against both God's Law and human logic?

## Saul and the Medium of En-dor (28:1–25)

When Saul learns the Philistines are preparing a full-scale attack against Israel, he seeks the Lord's will directly through the prophets, but God remains silent. So Saul disguises himself and asks a medium in En-dor to bring up Samuel from the dead.

### CLEAR THE CONFUSION

**Did Samuel really return from the dead?**

The vision that appeared to the medium (some translations use the word *witch* rather than *medium*) at En-dor was likely a demon. The text never specifically calls this apparition Samuel; rather, Saul calls it Samuel. Necromancy—communicating with or summoning the dead—was clearly forbidden by God, so it seems unlikely that God would allow it on this occasion.

How does Achish's difficult conversation with David demonstrate his honor and respect for David?

## The Philistines Reject David (29:1–11)

The Philistine armies gather to fight against the Israelites, but pressure Achish to send David away lest he turn against them in battle. David gives a show of protest, but the next morning leaves the Philistines to return to Ziklag. David will not be there for Saul's final battle.

## David's Wives Are Captured (30:1–15)

During David's absence, the Amalekites raided Ziklag, capturing all the women and children before burning the city. David and his men pursue the Amalekites. They find an Egyptian servant the Amalekites abandoned to die who promises to lead David to the Amalekites in return for safety.

## David Defeats the Amalekites (30:16–31)

David and his men raid the Amalekite camp, recovering all of the captured wives and children. As they return home, they meet two hundred of David's men who had remained behind from exhaustion. David insists that the spoils be shared among all his warriors.

## The Death of Saul (31:1–13)

The Philistines attack the Israelites, striking them down at Mount Gilboa. Three of Saul's sons including Jonathan are killed, and Saul is struck by Philistine archers. Knowing capture is imminent, Saul begs his armor-bearer to kill him. When he refuses, Saul falls on his own sword, killing himself.

### CLEAR THE CONFUSION

**Why did Saul kill himself?**

Saul feared the Philistines would torture and humiliate him as they had done when they captured Samson years before, so Saul took his own life. By this act, Saul showed his fear of the Philistines was greater than his fear of God. He would have been wiser to repent and entrust himself, body and soul, to God.

# 2 SAMUEL

## Welcome to 2 Samuel

The second half of the original book of Samuel traces David's kingship from Saul's death to nearly the end of David's reign. While David enjoys political advances and victories, his personal life is plagued with sin and conflict.

What parts of 2 Samuel are familiar to you? What are some specific things you'd like to learn more about?

## 2 Samuel at a Glance

- **Start:** The book of 2 Samuel begins with David learning of the death of King Saul.
- **End:** The book concludes with the final words of David as he approaches the end of his life.
- **Theme:** The book of 2 Samuel covers the reign of King David and the challenges he faces with his family.
- **Author and Date:** The author of 2 Samuel is unknown. The book was written as one book with 1 Samuel around 970 BC.
- **Places Visited:** Hebron, Jerusalem, and various battlefields
- **Journey Time:** The twenty-four chapters of 2 Samuel can be read in about two hours.
- **Outline:**
  - David Becomes King of Judah (1:1–4:12)
  - David Becomes King of All Israel (5:1–10:19)
  - David's Sin and Family Troubles (11:1–18:33)
  - David Is Restored and Completes His Reign (19:1–24:25)

## Five Top Sights and Spectacles of 2 Samuel

**Jerusalem Becomes the Capital (5:1–16)** Observe the consolidation of the nation as David makes Jerusalem the capital of a united Israel.

**David and Bathsheba (11:1–12:25)** Witness the sin that disrupts David's reign and the consequences that follow.

**David's Family Torn Apart (13:1–39)** Experience the sadness as sin and revenge tear David's family apart.

**Absalom's Rebellion (15:1–18:33)** Find out who will succeed as Absalom attempts to overthrow his father's throne.

**David's Last Words (23:1–7)** Listen as David gives his final public statement.

## Seeing Jesus in 2 Samuel

King David's reign foreshadows the coming of Jesus, our Savior and King. Jesus' earthly parents, Mary and Joseph, will be descendants of David. Jesus will even be born in Bethlehem, the city of David. David's reign, while far from perfect, gives us a small glimpse of the perfect reign of Jesus Christ and the glorious eternal kingdom that awaits all believers.

## David Becomes King of Judah (1:1–4:12)

After Saul's death, David returns to Israel and becomes the king of the tribe of Judah. Saul's son Ish-bosheth rules Israel. Over time, David grows stronger and Ish-bosheth weaker. Finally, Ish-bosheth is murdered.

Considering Saul's numerous attempts to kill David, how does David's reaction to the news of Saul's death surprise you?

### David Hears of Saul's Death (1:1–16)

An Amalekite comes to David carrying Saul's crown and armlet. He reports finding Saul on Mount Gilboa. The king begged him to end his life, and the man did. David and his men grieve the death of Saul and Jonathan. David executes the Amalekite for killing the anointed king.

**CLEAR THE CONFUSION**

**How did Saul really die?**

The account in 1 Samuel 31 states that Saul fell on his own sword, and died. But two possibilities follow. Either Saul did not instantly die and the Amalekite assisted his suicide or the Amalekite came across Saul's corpse and took his crown and armlet to David hoping to receive a reward. Whichever was the case, David took the Amalekite at his word and put him to death.

## David's Lament for Saul and Jonathan (1:17–27)

David records a lament over Saul and Jonathan in the Book of Jashar. He reminds Israel of the great victories and benefits Saul had won for them. At the same time, David warns Israel's enemies against gloating over Saul's death. He concludes with a personal word about Jonathan.

### CLEAR THE CONFUSION

**What is the Book of Jashar?**

The Book of Jashar was a collection of songs and poetic descriptions of historical events of ancient Israel. It was probably similar to the Psalms but contained Hebrew poetry focused on historical events. It was not preserved and has been lost to history.

## David Anointed King of Judah (2:1–7)

God directs David to Hebron, where the men of Judah anoint him as king. David brings along his wives and all of his men with their families. When he is informed that the men of Jabesh-gilead risked their lives to bury Saul's body, he blesses them for their kindness.

## Ish-bosheth Made King of Israel (2:8–11)

Abner, the leader of Saul's army, defies God's will by declaring Saul's son Ish-bosheth king over Israel. Mahanaim serves as Ish-bosheth's capital during his two-year reign.

## The Battle of Gibeon (2:12–32)

### VISUALIZE

The servants of Ish-bosheth and David met near Gibeon. The battle began with a face-off of twelve warriors from each side. When the twelve killed each other, a full-on battle broke out in which Ish-bosheth's men were beaten. In the battle, Abner killed Joab's brother Asahel after giving him fair warning.

How was warfare different at this time? Why might they have battled this way?

### Abner Joins David (3:1–25)

As the war between Saul's household and David continues, David grows stronger and Ish-bosheth weaker. When Ish-bosheth accuses Abner of trying to seize the kingdom, Abner offers to join David's side and convinces the elders of Israel to unite the nation under David.

### Joab Murders Abner (3:26–30)

Joab murders Abner to avenge his brother Asahel's death and assure his position as head of David's army. When David discovers Joab's action, he pronounces judgment against Joab's household but does not depose him.

### David Mourns Abner (3:31–39)

David declares a time of mourning for Abner, so the people weep and put on sackcloth. He refuses to eat, so all the people are impressed with David's actions and convinced he had no part in Abner's death.

Why was David displeased with Baanah and Rechab?

### Ish-bosheth Murdered (4:1–12)

When Ish-bosheth learns Abner is dead, his courage fails. Two of Israel's military captains, Baanah and Rechab, stab Ish-bosheth to death, cut off his head, and take it to David. Rather than being impressed and rewarding them, David orders his men to execute Baanah and Rechab.

**CLEAR THE CONFUSION**

**What about Mephibosheth?**

In the narrative of Ish-bosheth's murder, one verse describes Jonathan's son, Mephibosheth (v. 4). Suffering disabling injuries as a boy, Mephibosheth was unlikely to have been considered as a successor to Ish-bosheth. In 2 Samuel 9, we learn how David made special provisions for this son of his great friend.

## David Becomes King of All Israel (5:1–10:19)

After Ish-bosheth's murder, David is anointed king over all Israel. He captures Jerusalem and brings the ark of the covenant up into the city. He wins peace for Israel by defeating the neighboring nations in war.

## David Anointed King of Israel (5:1–16)

The tribes of Israel anoint David as king over Israel in Hebron. David captures Jerusalem and makes it his stronghold. Hiram, the king of Tyre, sends cedar wood and laborers to build a house for David. David's family grows as he adds wives, concubines, and many children.

? Why was King Hiram's decision to send cedar wood to David a wise one?

## David Defeats the Philistines (5:17–25)

The Philistines come against David at the Valley of Rephaim when they hear he has been made king over all Israel. The Lord gives David victory in his defense against their initial assault. Before the Philistines can strike again, God directs David to ambush them in a surprise attack to rout their army.

**VISUALIZE**

**Israel's Capital: Jerusalem**

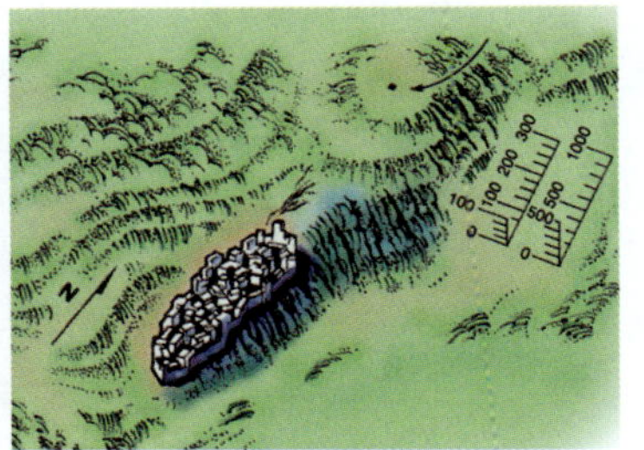

Jerusalem sat at the head of a valley with steep sides. The only easy way into the city was from the north. David's choice of Jerusalem for his capital was quite intentional. He knew the defensibility and central location of Jerusalem made the City of David, as it became known, an ideal capital city.

What additional information would you like to learn about Jerusalem?

## The Ark Brought to Jerusalem (6:1–4)

Having established Jerusalem as Israel's political center, David is determined to move the ark to Jerusalem to make the city the spiritual heart of the nation. David takes thirty thousand men to move the ark. They transport it on a new ox cart driven by Uzzah and Ahio.

## Uzzah and the Ark (6:5–15)

**WAYPOINT**

***What does this text show us?***

When the oxen pulling the cart stumble, Uzzah reaches out to steady the ark and God instantly strikes him down. Angry and fearful, David leaves the ark at the house of Obed-edom. When he sees God blesses Obed-edom's household, David sends Levites to carry the ark as Moses commanded.

Review 2 Samuel 6:5–15. Besides the obvious shock of Uzzah's death, what other things in this text surprise you?

How has God's judgment/mercy seat changed from the days of the ark of the covenant to today?

How can you learn more about the roles God has for you in the church?

***What does this text reveal about God's plan of salvation?***
The ark was the place where God was present among His people. Those places that housed the ark were often blessed through its presence. The ark pointed ahead to God's Son, who came to dwell among us. Now Jesus dwells in each believer, bringing blessings to the world through His presence.

***What does this text uncover about our identity and calling as God's people today?***
God calls each of us to specific roles in life and in the church. He uses these roles to benefit the church and the world. In worship, we as God's people can celebrate His Word and the great gift of Jesus, our Savior.

### CLEAR THE CONFUSION

**Why did God strike Uzzah down?**

Uzzah probably had the best intention when he reached out to steady the ark. But the ark symbolized God's holy presence which could not be touched by a sinner without immediate punishment. The ark was to be carried only by Levites using long poles so the ark itself would never be touched.

## David and Michal (6:16–23)

As the ark is carried into Jerusalem, David leaps and dances for joy before the Lord. When David's wife Michal sees his behavior, she despises her husband. As a result of her disdain, Michal never has any children.

## God's Covenant with David (7:1–17)

### WAYPOINT

Review the text of the Lord's covenant with David. What questions do you have about this text?

How does Jesus guide us as our Good Shepherd?

***What does this text show us?***
David tells the prophet Nathan he desires to construct a temple for God. Through Nathan, God tells David he is not the one to build the temple; instead, his son will build it. But God will build an eternal house for him; that is, one of David's descendants will be the promised Savior, the eternal King of Israel.

***What does this text reveal about God's plan of salvation?***
As a young man, David had served as the shepherd for his father, Jesse. As king, David shepherds God's chosen people as they build up the earthly kingdom. Now, Jesus is our Good Shepherd, and He leads His people to green pastures in the new heaven and new earth.

***What does this text uncover about our identity and calling as God's people today?***

Our Good Shepherd calls us to follow Him as His sheep. God gives us the opportunity to gather together in various places around the world and create houses of worship in those places. God uses our congregations to reach out into our communities with the good news of the Gospel.

List some ways your congregation could reach out in your community. How can you serve others?

## David's Prayer of Gratitude (7:18–29)

Having God's promise through the prophet Nathan, David responds in a prayer of thanksgiving. David acknowledges his unworthiness of everything God has done for him. David expresses amazement at God choosing his descendants to bring the promised Messiah to the world.

## David's Victories (8:1–14)

David defeats the Philistines, Moab, and Hadadezer of Zobah. When the Syrians come to help Zobah, David's men defeat them. When Toi, the king of Hamath, hears of David's victories over Hadadezer, his enemy, he wisely sends his son to make a peace alliance with David.

## David's Officials (8:15–18)

David appoints a number of men to responsibilities within the kingdom. These include leaders over the army, priests, a recorder, and a secretary.

## David's Kindness to Mephibosheth (9:1–13)

David questions Ziba, a former servant from the household of King Saul, concerning any remaining descendants of Saul. Ziba tells him about Jonathan's son, Mephibosheth. Out of respect for his friend Jonathan, David invites Mephibosheth to eat at his table for the rest of his life.

How does David's choice to care for Mephibosheth reflect his character and his relationship with Jonathan?

### LINK BETWEEN THE TESTAMENTS

**David Invites Mephibosheth to His Table → Jesus Invites Us to His Table (2 Samuel 9:10 → Matthew 26:26–29; Luke 22:14–20)**

Upon learning about Jonathan's son, David invites Mephibosheth to eat at his table. Responding to Mephibosheth's humble response (v. 8), David assures Mephibosheth that this invitation is genuine, and Mephibosheth continues to dine at the king's table.

As Jesus instituted the Lord's Supper when He gathered His disciples to celebrate the Passover, He looked ahead to us. We are "dead dogs" in our sin, yet we have a seat at the Lord's Table, where He feeds us with His very body and blood for the forgiveness of sins.

### David Defeats Ammon and Syria (10:1–19)

How does Joab's battle plan work? Why does it turn out to be so successful?

When the king of the Ammonites dies, David sends servants to his son, Hanun, to offer comfort. Hanun suspects these men are spies and treats them disgracefully. Realizing his error and fearing David's wrath, Hanun hires Syrian warriors to help defend them. Joab routs both armies.

## David's Sin and Family Troubles (11:1–18:33)

David sees a beautiful woman, commits adultery with her, and murders her husband. God announces through the prophet Nathan that David's household will be filled with violence. David's children suffer rape, murder for revenge, and launch a coup to seize David's kingdom.

### David and Bathsheba (11:1–27)

**VISUALIZE**

From his palace roof, David sees a beautiful woman bathing on her rooftop. He sends for her and commits adultery with her. When she sends him word she is pregnant, David has her husband brought home from battle, thinking he will sleep with his wife and believe the child is his. When all efforts fail, David sends the husband back with orders for Joab.

### Nathan Rebukes David (12:1–15a)

**WAYPOINT**

Reread the verses in this section. What surprises do you find?

***What does this text show us?***

God sends Nathan the prophet to confront David for his sin. Nathan tells David a story that makes David respond in outrage and see his own guilt. When David repents, he is forgiven, but Nathan tells of the consequences that will follow.

***What does this text reveal about God's plan of salvation?***
Just as Nathan reassured David, so we receive the same good news. The Lord has put aside our sins and removed the punishment of eternal death through the suffering, death, and resurrection of our Savior, Jesus Christ.

***What does this text uncover about our identity and calling as God's people today?***
Just as Nathan confronted David, God's Law confronts us for our sin. In worship, we confess those sins and are assured of God's complete forgiveness through the Words of Absolution. Like David, we may bear earthly consequences for our sinful decisions, but God's forgiveness carries us through.

Nathan reassured David of God's mercy and forgiveness. Where do we hear that same message?

Why is truthfulness so important for all believers?

## David's Child Dies (12:15b–23)

Immediately, David suffers the first consequence for his sin. When his newborn child becomes sick, David fasts and prays, but on the seventh day, the child dies. David amazes his servants and makes a great confession of faith in God's forgiveness and eternal life.

## Solomon's Birth (12:24–25)

David comforts Bathsheba, and she becomes pregnant. The birth of their son Solomon (whose name means "peace") brings great joy to them both. The prophet Nathan gives their son a second name, Jedidiah, which means "beloved of Yahweh," which is a play on *David* ("beloved").

## Rabbah Is Captured (12:26–31)

Joab sends a message to David that he will soon capture the royal city of the Ammonites. Joab invites David to finalize the defeat of Rabbah, which he does. The golden crown now adorns David's head. The captives are forced to destroy their own city and make bricks for Israel.

## Amnon and Tamar (13:1–22)

Likely encouraged by his father's adultery, David's eldest son, Amnon, lusts after his half-sister, Tamar. After raping her, Amnon despises her and casts her out. Absalom takes Tamar into his home and informs the king. Though David is filled with anger, he does not discipline Amnon.

Consider how we might react to this type of situation today. What legal and social issues would result?

### CLEAR THE CONFUSION

**Why did Tamar urge Amnon to speak with David to take her as his wife?**

Tamar likely hoped their father (David) or Absalom would protect her from Amnon's advances. Tamar knew that losing her virginity would forever bring shame on David and his house. When Amnon thrust her out after raping her, he insinuated that Tamar was at fault, and her reputation was destroyed.

## Absalom Murders Amnon (13:23–33)

Another consequence of David's sin comes two years after Tamar's rape. Absalom, Tamar's full brother, has acted civilly toward Amnon, while secretly plotting revenge against him. He invites King David and all his sons to join in a sheepshearing celebration where he will exact revenge.

## Absalom Flees to Geshur (13:34–39)

As the rest of the king's sons return to David, Absalom flees. For the next three years, Absalom lives in Geshur with his mother's father. King David spends that time longing to bring Absalom home, either to forgive him or to punish him. But David does nothing.

### CLEAR THE CONFUSION

**Why did David do nothing when Amnon raped Tamar or when Absalom murdered Amnon?**

David was an excellent king but an absentee father. With so many children through so many wives, he likely left the mothers to raise their children and didn't involve himself as he should. David's inaction after Tamar's rape alienated Absalom from his father, who refused to give Tamar justice.

## Absalom Returns to Jerusalem (14:1–33)

Read 2 Samuel 14 again. How is the act designed by Joab similar to the story Nathan used to confront David about Bathsheba?

### WAYPOINT

***What does this text show us?***

Prompted by Joab, David brings Absalom back to Jerusalem but does not see him. After spending two years in Jerusalem without being summoned to his father, Absalom finally forces Joab to bring him to his father, and David publicly shows his forgiveness and restoration by kissing his son.

***What does this text reveal about God's plan of salvation?***
Absalom has murdered his own brother and desperately needs the mercy and grace of God. God demonstrates that same mercy to us. He sent His Son to earn our forgiveness even while we are still His enemies. His undeserved grace is shown through Christ's death and resurrection.

How and where do we cry out for mercy to God regarding our sins?

***What does this text uncover about our identity and calling as God's people today?***
Despite our sinfulness, God forgives our sins for the sake of His Son. Just as David's kiss sealed his forgiveness of Absalom, Christ's gifts of Baptism and Communion seal His forgiveness to us. Since we are forgiven by the Father, we are called to forgive those who sin against us.

Where are we regularly reminded of our status as God's forgiven children?

## Absalom's Conspiracy (15:1–12)

Completely alienated from his father, Absalom gets a chariot and horses and gathers fifty men to accompany him. Daily, he intercepts all who are coming to David to resolve disputes and convinces them the king will not listen to them; after all, David did nothing after Amnon raped Tamar.

## David Flees Jerusalem (15:13–37)

**VISUALIZE**

David receives word that Absalom has turned the hearts of the men of Israel to himself. Fearing for the safety of his family, David flees the city with all his household and servants. He leaves behind ten concubines to maintain the house. At the Mount of Olives, David learns his trusted adviser Ahithophel has betrayed him to support Absalom.

## CLEAR THE CONFUSION

How did these faithful Philistines foreshadow the inclusion of Gentiles in the Christian Church?

**Who were the Cherethites, Pelethites, and Gittites? Why do they get special mention here?**

These were Philistine warriors who had allied themselves with David and remained faithful to him when most of Israel turned to Absalom. The Gittites came from Gath, the home of Goliath. Now, some of David's most faithful followers were people from Goliath's hometown.

## LINK BETWEEN THE TESTAMENTS

**Ahithophel Betrays David → Judas Betrays Jesus (2 Samuel 15:31 → John 13:25–27; 18:2–5)**

David had a trusted adviser named Ahithophel. Ahithophel ate at David's table and had David's intimate trust. Learning that Ahithophel betrayed him and was likely the architect of Absalom's conspiracy was devastating to David.

Jesus chose Judas Iscariot as one of His twelve disciples—those eating, drinking, and talking with Jesus during His public ministry. Judas sat at the table at the Last Supper feigning loyalty and love. Then, when he led the soldiers to this same Mount of Olives to arrest Jesus, he betrayed Him with a kiss.

## CLEAR THE CONFUSION

**Why did David choose to flee instead of fighting Absalom's uprising?**

David's decision to flee Jerusalem may seem unusual, but he took into consideration the safety of his household and the families of his supporters. Staying in Jerusalem put everyone at risk of being trapped in a besieged city. Instead of facing these dangers, David wisely chose to abandon the capital.

## David and Ziba (16:1–4)

Mephibosheth's servant Ziba arrives with food loaded onto two donkeys. Ziba pledges his support to David and explains that Mephibosheth has remained behind in Jerusalem, convinced that Absalom will restore the kingdom to Saul's household. Ziba pledges his loyalty to David.

## CLEAR THE CONFUSION

**Was Ziba telling the truth about Mephibosheth?**

Most biblical scholars doubt the truth of Ziba's statement. With the extent of Mephibosheth's injuries, who would want to make him king? Certainly not Absalom, who wanted the throne for himself. It seems more likely that Ziba concocted this story to gain support from David and seize his master's property.

## Shimei Curses David (16:5–14)

Shimei, a relative of Saul, follows David as he flees, cursing David while throwing stones and dirt at him. David's nephew Abishai offers to cut off Shimei's head, but David restrains him. As David and his men continue on toward the Jordan, Shimei follows along, cursing him the entire way.

## Absalom Enters Jerusalem (16:15–23)

Absalom enters Jerusalem. Ahithophel, King David's former counselor, advises Absalom to publicly sleep with David's concubines, thus making himself a "stench" (v. 21) to his father—that is, Absalom is publicly claiming David's place as king over Israel.

## Hushai Saves David (17:1–29)

Ahithophel advises Absalom to pursue David immediately, strike him down, and avoid needless war. Hushai, a counselor David had sent back to ruin Ahithophel's counsel, convinces Absalom to wait and gather the whole army of Israel against David.

What difference do you see between the way David deals with advice and the way Absalom deals with advice?

## CLEAR THE CONFUSION

**Why did Ahithophel kill himself?**

Ahithophel knew Absalom's only chance to hold the kingdom was to quickly assassinate David while his forces were in retreat. Hushai's plan gave David time to recover himself and organize his forces for victory. Since defeat was now certain, Ahithophel set his house in order and hanged himself.

The parallels between Judas and Ahithophel are striking. Both betrayed their kings; both were filled with remorse. But instead of repenting and seeking forgiveness, they both hanged themselves.

## Absalom Killed (18:1–18)

### VISUALIZE

When have you done something you knew was wrong because you thought the end would justify the means?

As David's forces go out to battle, David orders his commanders to deal gently with Absalom. In the battle, Absalom's army suffers great losses. When he attempts to flee on his mule, his long hair becomes entangled in the branches of an oak tree. Joab disobeys David and kills him.

### LINK BETWEEN THE TESTAMENTS

**Absalom → Jesus**
**(2 Samuel 18:9 → Matthew 21:1–11; 27:32–35)**

In Israel, kings and their families rode on mules. Absalom rode on a mule to claim he was now the king of Israel. When he was caught by his hair in the oak tree, God dethroned him, exposing him as a fraud. Hanging suspended between heaven and earth from a tree, he was cursed and killed.

In the Gospels, Jesus rode a donkey into Jerusalem on the Sunday before His death and resurrection, showing He was indeed the King of Israel. On Good Friday, He was raised up on a cross, hanging from a tree, suspended in the breach between God and sinful humanity. He bore the curse of our sins and suffered and died in our place.

### CLEAR THE CONFUSION

**Why did Joab defy David's command and strike down Absalom?**

Joab had watched David refuse to do anything about Amnon's rape of Tamar or Absalom's murder of Amnon. He feared David would not hold Absalom accountable for his sinful rebellion. Joab previously had killed Abner in retaliation (2 Samuel 3). He was not above using murder to accomplish his goals.

### David Hears of Absalom's Death (18:19–30)

Joab sends a Cushite to report on the victory because he knows David will be unhappy about Absalom's death. Ahimaaz the priest gets to David first and reports the victory. When David asks about Absalom, Ahimaaz loses his nerve and claims he does not know, although he does.

How do we grieve today? How is it different from the grieving process in biblical times?

### David's Grief (18:31–33)

The Cushite arrives and tells David about the victory and Absalom's death. David retreats to his room and cries out in grief. David clearly feels the full weight and responsibility for all the evil that has occurred in his family. His grief overwhelms him.

## David Is Restored and Completes His Reign (19:1–24:25)

David returns to Jerusalem to resume his reign. After foolishly ordering a census for which Israel is punished, he purchases a threshing floor to offer a sacrifice. On this site, the plague is stopped and Solomon will build the temple.

### Joab Rebukes David (19:1–8a)

Joab rebukes the king for his excessive grieving. David finally realizes he is mourning as if God had abandoned him, and he is rejecting God's call for him to be king. David emerges from his chambers and takes his seat by the gate, publicly resuming his role as king.

### David Returns to Jerusalem (19:8b–15)

Absalom is dead, but no one is bringing David back to Jerusalem. Through the priests, David sends word to the leaders of Judah that they should be the ones to bring him back and restore him to his throne. The people of Jerusalem gladly welcome David back.

#### CLEAR THE CONFUSION

**Why did David vow to replace Joab as commander of Israel's army with Amasa?**

David knew that Joab had murdered Abner in cold blood and likely suspected Joab had killed Absalom. Also, since Absalom had placed Amasa over the army of Israel, by replacing Joab with Amasa, David could clearly show Israel he would not retaliate against those who had joined Absalom.

## David Pardons His Enemies (19:16–43)

Shimei, the relative of Saul, hurries to apologize to David as he crosses over the Jordan. David promises Shimei he will not be put to death. Mephibosheth comes to David and tells him Ziba had deceived him. David divides the household of Saul between Ziba and Mephibosheth.

## The Rebellion of Sheba (20:1–26)

**WAYPOINT**

Read through chapter 20 concerning Sheba's rebellion. What questions do you have about this event?

Where can we turn for reassurance of God's forgiveness?

How can we express our thankfulness for God's gift of forgiveness and salvation?

***What does this text show us?***
A man named Sheba, from the tribe of Benjamin, tries to divide Israel and restore the kingship to Saul's tribe. David directs Amasa to stop him, but Amasa delays, so David sends Abishai, Joab's brother. Joab and Amasa meet on the road.

***What does this text reveal about God's plan of salvation?***
Despite the violence that continues to plague David's reign, his restoration demonstrates the dependability of God's promise to bring forth the Savior from the lineage of David.

***What does this text uncover about our identity and calling as God's people today?***
God calls us to repentance and restores us through Jesus Christ. He uses the wisdom and work of those around us to demonstrate His desire for our lives. Our lives reflect the gift of salvation that is ours through the death and resurrection of Christ.

## David Avenges the Gibeonites (21:1–14)

After the land suffers a three-year famine, God reveals to David that Saul broke Joshua's covenant with the Gibeonites (Joshua 9) by attempting to destroy them. David asks the Gibeonites how he can rectify this offense.

### CLEAR THE CONFUSION

**Wasn't Mephibosheth protected by David? Why did God allow these descendants of Saul to be killed?**

Note that there are two men named Mephibosheth in this account: one is the son of Jonathan, the other is Saul's son through a concubine. David protected Jonathan's son, but Saul's son died at the hand of the Gibeonites.

The death of Saul's sons and grandsons was the penalty for his violation of Israel's covenant under Joshua. God does not let sin go unpunished, as we see in the great suffering and death our Lord Jesus Christ accepted in our place.

## War with the Philistines (21:15–22)

David and his men fight the Philistines again. When David grows tired, a Philistine giant targets him, but Joab's brother Abishai kills the giant. In three subsequent battles, David's men kill three more Philistine giants, including the brother of Goliath, whom David had killed in his youth.

### SET THE SCENE

**Who are the giants?**

God promised the land of the giants ("Rephaim" in Hebrew) to Abraham (see Genesis 15:18–21). The Philistine giant Goliath of Gath, whom young David defeated, was a descendant of the Rephaim. Clearly such gigantic warriors would have been natural champions among the Philistine soldiers.

## David's Song of Deliverance (22:1–51)

### WAYPOINT

***What does this text show us?***
David records his song of deliverance from his enemies. Note that this song appears as the eighteenth psalm in the book of Psalms. The song was likely written some time after the defeat of Sheba, since David refers to the defeat of all his enemies.

***What does this text reveal about God's plan of salvation?***
David repeatedly praises God for how the Lord rescued him from his enemies. Christ rescues us from the enemies of sin, death, and Satan, not because we deserve rescue but because God is faithful and gracious.

Read through David's song of deliverance once again. What one or two phrases could you commit to memory?

What great reassurance concerning our salvation do we read in this section of Scripture?

What does it mean to you that you are God's chosen child?

***What does this text uncover about our identity and calling as God's people today?***

As God's chosen people, beloved and forgiven, we respond to God's care and mercy by giving Him our praise and loving our neighbor. Like David, we do not deserve God's goodness, but He freely gives it to us anyway. As we live our lives in the world today, we can share that good news with others around us.

## The Last Words of David (23:1–7)

David speaks his last recorded words. Some commentators call this oracle David's last will and testament. David sums up his life as the psalmist (hymn writer) of Israel. The Spirit of God speaks through David to prosper everything David does.

## David's Mighty Men (23:8–39)

David lists his elite warriors. It includes "the three," mighty men who excelled in their service to David and Israel. Next are the thirty and their two leaders. Note that Joab is not listed here, though his brother Abishai is head of the thirty. The last of the thirty is Bathsheba's husband Uriah the Hittite, the man David had murdered.

## David's Census (24:1–9)

In pride, David orders a census of all those eligible for military service. Joab rightly asks David to reconsider, but David's word prevails. After nine months and twenty days, Joab reports the results of the census. Israel comprises 800,000 valiant men, while Judah has 500,000 men.

## The LORD's Judgment of David's Sin (24:10–17)

After the census, David feels great guilt and pleads with God for forgiveness. God sends the prophet Gad to announce three possible consequences for David's sin from which David must choose. As pestilence rages across Israel, David sees the Angel of the Lord nearing Jerusalem.

### CLEAR THE CONFUSION

**Who was this Angel of the Lord?**

This sword-wielding Angel reminds the reader of the Angel of the Lord who appeared in Joshua 5:13–15. Biblical commentaries suggest that this was, in fact, an appearance of the preincarnate Christ. When David addressed the Angel, he was speaking directly to the Second Person of the Trinity.

Use a Bible search tool to find other times the Angel of the Lord appeared. Where else do we see these appearances of the preincarnate Christ?

## David Builds an Altar (24:18–25)

### VISUALIZE

The prophet Gad came to David at Araunah's threshing floor and directed him to raise an altar and make a sacrifice. When David asked to purchase the threshing floor, Araunah offered to give David the land as well as the oxen for the sacrifice and the yokes as wood for the fire. David refused Araunah's generous offer and instead purchased the land from him.

### SET THE SCENE

**What was the significance of this threshing floor?**

Araunah's threshing floor was located on Mount Moriah where God told Abraham to offer up his son Isaac in Genesis 22:2. In this text, David purchased this site to build an altar to sacrifice to the Lord. David's son Solomon will later build the temple of the Lord at this same site on Mount Moriah.

# 1 KINGS

## Welcome to 1 Kings

What kings are you familiar with after Saul and David? What are some specific things you'd like to learn more about?

In the Hebrew Bible, the contents of 1 and 2 Kings were written on a single scroll. These books relate Israel's history from the end of David's reign through the division of Israel into two kingdoms and the fall and exile of both of those kingdoms. As you read through 1 Kings, notice God's great patience for His wayward people and notice the prophets He raises to call them back to Him. In much the same way, He now calls you and me through the Law and Gospel in His Holy Scriptures.

## 1 Kings at a Glance

- **Start:** The book of 1 Kings begins with David appointing Solomon to succeed him.
- **End:** The book concludes with the ministry of the prophet Elijah.
- **Theme:** The book of 1 Kings shows the division of Israel into two kingdoms, each of which God judges according to the faithfulness of each king.
- **Author and Date:** The author of 1 Kings is unknown. It was likely composed around 560 BC.
- **Places Visited:** Jerusalem, Samaria
- **Journey Time:** The twenty-two chapters of 1 Kings can be read in approximately two hours.
- **Outline:**
  - David's Reign Ends (1:1–2:12)
  - Solomon's Reign and Disobedience (2:13–11:43)
  - Division of the Kingdom of Israel and Jeroboam's Reign (12:1–14:20)
  - Kings of Israel and Judah and the Prophet Elijah (14:21–22:53)

# Five Top Sights and Spectacles of 1 Kings

**Solomon Builds the Temple (5:1–7:51)** Watch Solomon construct and furnish the temple in Jerusalem.

**The Kingdom of Israel Divided (12:1–24)** See ten of the tribes rebel against Solomon's son Rehoboam and form their own kingdom.

**Jeroboam I Reigns in Israel (12:25–14:20)** Watch God establish Jeroboam as Israel's first king and Jeroboam turn Israel away from the Lord.

**Ahab Reigns in Israel (16:29–22:40)** Observe the most evil and faithless king wreak havoc in the Northern Kingdom.

**Elijah the Prophet Ministers in Israel (17:1–21:29)** Notice God raising up one of the greatest prophets of the Old Testament when things are most bleak in the northern kingdom.

# Seeing Jesus in 1 Kings

Israel's kings give us a glimpse of the reign of Jesus Christ. Not a single king of Israel follows God wholeheartedly, but many in Judah honor God's covenant and seek to worship rightly at the temple. The temple is a powerful image of Jesus, who offered Himself for all our sins.

# David's Reign Ends (1:1–2:12)

David has grown very weak in his old age. His son Adonijah proclaims himself king without David's knowledge. When the prophet Nathan and Bathsheba tell David of the coup, he makes clear who his successor will be.

## David in His Old Age (1:1–4)

In his final years, David's vitality is so drained he is unable to keep warm. His servants search for a beautiful young virgin to serve him and lay alongside him. A girl named Abishag the Shunammite is chosen. She sleeps beside David, but they do not have marital relations.

## Adonijah Sets Himself Up as King (1:5–10)

Adonijah, David's oldest surviving son, follows in Absalom's path, getting a chariot and fifty attendants to run ahead of him. When David does not interfere, he recruits David's commander Joab and one of David's two chief priests, Abiathar, to stand beside him as he proclaims himself king.

When have you been tempted to claim authority or power that is not yours to claim?

## Nathan and Bathsheba Before David (1:11–27)

Bathsheba, Solomon's mother, asks David if he has chosen Adonijah to be king instead of Solomon. Bathsheba reminds David that he swore Solomon would succeed him. While Bathsheba is with David, Nathan asks David if he has indeed chosen Adonijah to be his successor.

## Solomon Anointed King (1:28–53)

David affirms his vow to Bathsheba and directs his officials—Zadok the priest, the military commander Benaiah, and Nathan the prophet—to have Solomon ride David's own mule, immediately anoint Solomon as king, and then bring him to David's throne.

**PICTURE OF THE SAVIOR**

**The Son of David Rode a Mule into Jerusalem**

Israel frequently saw David the king riding on a mule. When they saw Solomon riding that same mule, they knew he was David's choice to succeed him as king. On the Sunday before Jesus' death and resurrection, He rode into Jerusalem on a donkey. This clear claim of kingship resulted in the crowds' praises.

What are some things leaders use today to identify themselves as leaders?

## David's Instructions to Solomon (2:1–9)

David admonishes Solomon to be faithful to the Lord and to closely obey Moses' commands. Then he directs Solomon to punish Joab and Shimei, two individuals who wronged David and incurred blood guilt but had not faced any consequences up to this point.

### The Death of David (2:10–12)

After reigning over Judah and Israel for forty years, David dies and is buried in Jerusalem. Solomon reigns in his place, and Solomon's kingdom is firmly established against any of the other sons of David who might have thought they should rule in his place.

**CLEAR THE CONFUSION**

**What does the phrase "David slept with his fathers" in verse 10 signify?**

David's earthly life ended in death. But the Holy Spirit inspired the writer to use *sleep* instead of *death* to teach both Old and New Testament believers that death is not the end of our existence. Through God's promised Savior, all believers will be awakened and restored to life when Jesus Christ returns.

## Solomon's Reign and Disobedience (2:13–11:43)

After receiving keen discernment and wisdom from God, Solomon builds the temple and Israel enjoys great wealth and fame. But Solomon marries hundreds of women who lead him into idolatry. God announces that He will tear ten tribes away from Solomon's son Rehoboam.

Our sinful nature likes to be in control and to secure our positions in life. What are some ways you have found to place that control and security into Jesus' hands?

### Solomon's Reign Established (2:13–46)

This passage shows how Solomon dealt with four men who threatened his rule. He shows his wisdom by recognizing their threats and treating the men according to their actions.

**CLEAR THE CONFUSION**

**Why was Adonijah's request to marry Abishag seen as treason?**

In that time, a man who claimed the throne slept with the former king's concubines to show the world he was taking the king's place (see 2 Samuel 16:20–23). Adonijah's request to marry Abishag revealed his desire to usurp Solomon's throne.

**Was Solomon morally right to execute Adonijah, Joab, and Shimei?**

Each of these men had committed sins that by the Law of Moses were punishable by death, but David had spared them. In his wisdom Solomon gave each man a condition by which he could live peaceably and avoid execution, but each broke Solomon's conditions, resulting in their death.

## Solomon's Prayer for Wisdom (3:1–15)

Solomon loves the Lord and offers sacrifices at the high place in Gibeon. God appears to him in a dream, inviting him to make a request. Solomon asks for discernment to rightly govern God's people. God gives him wisdom and discernment, and the wealth and fame he has not requested along with it.

Solomon prayed for discernment. What is the connection between discernment and wisdom? How can God's gift of discernment guard your life?

### CLEAR THE CONFUSION

**Why did Solomon offer these sacrifices at the high place instead of before the ark of the covenant in Jerusalem?**

In the days of Eli the priest, the ark had been taken out of the tabernacle (1 Samuel 4) and the two remained separated until Solomon built the temple and placed both the ark and the tabernacle inside. While the ark was in Jerusalem at this time, the tabernacle was at the high place in Gibeon.

**Why did Solomon marry the daughter of Pharaoh (3:1)?**

Political marriages were a common practice among rulers at the time. Since Pharaoh's daughter was living in Israel, Pharaoh would not be likely to attack his own daughter. Additionally, since Solomon's wife was from Egypt, Israel would be unlikely to attack Egypt, his wife's country.

## Solomon's Wisdom (3:16–28)

When two prostitutes each claim a living child is theirs, Solomon wisely and perceptively solves the matter by letting the true mother reveal herself. This news puts the people in awe of Solomon, who has the wisdom of God.

## Solomon's Officials (4:1–19)

Solomon divides Israel into twelve administrative districts. The first officials rule with him in Jerusalem; the twelve who follow are leaders stationed within their respective regions.

## Solomon's Wealth and Wisdom (4:20–34)

The empire of David's son Solomon is vast—the territory God had promised to Abraham. The Israelites enjoy great wealth and prosperity as well. These are the golden days for the people of Israel.

### CLEAR THE CONFUSION

**Do we still have any of Solomon's psalms or songs?**

Solomon wrote Psalms 72 and 127, as well as the book of Song of Solomon (also known as "Song of Songs," that is, the greatest song Solomon wrote).

## Preparations for Building the Temple (5:1–18)

Solomon arranges with Hiram, the king of Tyre, to buy cedar and cypress lumber in exchange for wheat and olive oil. Solomon also drafts laborers from the Canaanite descendants living among the Israelites to work with the timber and to quarry large stones out of the hill country of Israel.

How do the furnishings of your church building reflect God's glory and majesty?

## Solomon Builds the Temple (6:1–38)

A detailed description of the temple construction shows the lavish care, time, and expense Solomon gives to provide a dwelling place for God among the people of Israel in Jerusalem.

## Solomon Builds His Palace (7:1–12)

Solomon builds three structures for his dwelling. He will rule Israel from the Hall of the Throne. Though we don't know how he uses the House of the Forest of Lebanon or the Hall of Pillars, they are also clearly impressive structures.

### SET THE SCENE

**What stands out about Solomon's palace complex?**

Some of Solomon's buildings were larger than the Lord's temple and took him twice as long to build as it took to build the temple. Sadly, this indicates Solomon's priorities were shifting from seeking the glory of the Lord to seeking his own.

## The Temple Furnishings (7:13–51)

Solomon builds two massive bronze columns to hold up the portico at the temple's entrance; the large bronze sea for ceremonial washing; and other basins, shovels, and pots. All the furnishings inside the temple are gold, while those in the courtyard outside the temple are bronze.

## The Ark Brought into the Temple (8:1–11)

**WAYPOINT**

***What does this text show us?***
The priests carry the ark into the temple that Solomon built. The cloud of the Lord's glory fills the temple, showing God's presence dwelling in the temple.

***What does this text reveal about God's plan of salvation?***
When Moses set up the tabernacle on Mount Sinai, the glory of the Lord filled it to show that God was dwelling with His people. Now, God's glory dwells in the temple. These point ahead to God becoming human and dwelling with us in His Son, Jesus Christ.

***What does this text uncover about our identity and calling as God's people today?***
As we are washed in His blood, our Savior Jesus promises to be with us always, wherever we go. We are God's chosen people, set here to glorify God by sharing the good news of salvation in Jesus Christ through loving words and deeds to the people God has brought into our lives.

Where are other places in Scripture you have seen this glory of the Lord?

How is Jesus uniting His body and blood to the bread and wine in Holy Communion similar to the glory of the Lord entering the temple?

How does each Christian serve as a "temple" of God in the world?

## Solomon Blesses the LORD (8:12–21)

Solomon reminds the people of David's desire to build the temple and God's promise that David's son would build it. He praises God, who has humbled Himself to dwell in this temple among His people and yet is unsearchable, for keeping that promise.

## Solomon's Prayer of Dedication (8:22–53)

Solomon asks the Lord to listen to the prayers His people offer toward this temple, forgive their sins, and restore them. He names seven scenarios in which they may call out to Him. Solomon asks God to send His salvation out to all peoples of the earth through the Israelites (v. 43).

Describe a time in your life when it appeared that God had abandoned you but, in fact, He had been there the whole time.

**How did this prayer encourage Israelites of later generations?**

The books of 1 and 2 Kings culminate in the destruction of the temple and a remnant of Israel taken into exile in Babylon. Yet even from that exile, God's people cried out with confidence that God would hear and answer their prayer. This is what Daniel would do in Daniel 9, recalling this prayer of Solomon.

## Solomon's Benediction (8:54–61)

Solomon turns to bless the people. He calls on them to bless the Lord, to pray for Him to keep their hearts inclined to obey Him, and to be faithful.

## Solomon's Sacrifices (8:62–66)

Solomon offers an enormous number of peace offerings. These feed the people of Israel, who gather in Jerusalem for seven days for the dedication of the temple and the Feast of Booths.

## The LORD Appears to Solomon (9:1–9)

The Lord repeats the promises of His covenant with David and warns of the consequences for Solomon or his sons if they break that covenant. They must avoid the temptation to think that God will never let His temple be destroyed and that it will permanently guarantee their safety.

## Solomon's Other Acts (9:10–28)

We read a list of Solomon's accomplishments. Some are done to God's glory, others are done for Solomon's own greed and selfishness. All of Solomon's forced laborers are Canaanite survivors; not a single Israelite is enslaved to do his construction work.

## The Queen of Sheba (10:1–13)

Hearing of Solomon's reputation, the queen of Sheba comes to interview him. Her notable visit shows the powerful reputation God gave Solomon and also gives us a glimpse at how the reputation of God spreads from person to person and nation to nation for Jesus' sake.

## Solomon's Great Wealth (10:14–29)

Solomon truly enjoys a golden empire. God showers material possessions on him, and he accumulates gold, horses, and wives. This is the beginning of his fall from God.

How can we escape the temptation of putting our trust in material possessions?

**CLEAR THE CONFUSION**

**How did Solomon ignore God's prior warnings?**

In Deuteronomy 17:14–17, Moses powerfully anticipated the events recorded for us in 1 and 2 Kings. His warnings were to save the Israelites from turning away and falling under God's wrath. It was as though God had been speaking directly to Solomon, but wise Solomon was too foolish to listen to his God.

## Solomon Turns from the LORD (11:1–8)

Solomon does not listen to God's Word in the Law of Moses, which warned the Israelites not to marry foreign women. His many wives from political marriages turn his heart from the Lord to other gods. He builds altars and high places to these false gods.

Solomon became overconfident in his wisdom. Instead of humbling himself and trusting God, he broke the rules and learned the hard way. What directions from God do you find hard to trust?

**CLEAR THE CONFUSION**

**Why didn't God take away Solomon's kingdom as He took away Saul's?**

God preserved David's line because of David's faith and, even more importantly, because of His promise to send the Messiah through David's line (2 Samuel 7). For David's sake, and for the sake of God's eternal promise of the Christ, God did not snatch the entire kingdom from David's line because of Solomon's sin.

## The LORD Raises Adversaries (11:9–43)

The Lord announces He will tear the kingdom from Solomon's son and give it to one of his servants. Solomon will be plagued by adversaries during the remainder of his reign. God sends the prophet Ahijah to prophesy that God will give ten tribes to Jeroboam, the son of Nebat.

# Division of the Kingdom of Israel and Jeroboam's Reign (12:1–14:20)

When Solomon dies, his son Rehoboam rules Israel. Ten tribes abandon him and follow Jeroboam. Not trusting God to maintain his reign, Jeroboam builds two golden calves in Israel and chooses priests from other tribes to keep his people from going to the temple in Jerusalem.

When have you been tempted to assert your authority by answering someone harshly?

## Rehoboam's Folly (12:1–15)

When Rehoboam, Solomon's son, becomes king, Jeroboam stands before him representing the other Israelite tribes. He asks Rehoboam to lighten the heavy tax load Solomon had placed upon Israel. Rehoboam accepts the counsel of his young advisers and answers the Israelites harshly.

## The Kingdom Divided (12:16–24)

When Rehoboam foolishly refuses to negotiate with Jeroboam, ten of the tribes rebel and elect Jeroboam their king. When one of Rehoboam's representatives is stoned to death, he flees to Jerusalem and prepares his soldiers to retake control over Israel.

## Jeroboam's Golden Calves (12:25–33)

What is a fear that holds you back from trusting God's promises for your life?

Why do you think people want to invent their own ways to approach God?

When do you find yourself tempted to rely on your own works to be right with God?

**WAYPOINT**

***What does this text show us?***

Fearing his people will return to the throne of David when they go to the Jerusalem temple, Jeroboam builds two golden calves. He rejects God's chosen Levites, appointing his own priests from different tribes. This sinful practice will persist through all the kings of Israel until the nation is destroyed.

***What does this text reveal about God's plan of salvation?***

God alone has the authority to establish how sinners can come to Him. For His Old Testament people, He established Solomon's temple. In the New Testament, God established His Son, Jesus Christ, as the one mediator between God and humanity (see John 14:6).

***What does this text uncover about our identity and calling as God's people today?***

Jesus calls believers the light and salt of the earth. That is because we know Jesus is our only Savior from sin and death. It is urgent for us to share the Good News of Jesus Christ with the people God has brought into our lives, because He alone can give them salvation.

**SET THE SCENE**

**Why did Jeroboam choose golden calves?**

Jeroboam defied God's command for all Israel to worship at the temple under the Levitical priests, who were descendants of Aaron. He built golden calves, taking Israel back to the time Aaron built the golden calf at Mount Sinai. Perhaps Jeroboam was trying to relive Israel's newfound freedom from slavery.

## A Man of God Confronts Jeroboam (13:1–10)

God sends a prophet from Judah to warn Jeroboam and the people of Israel that He is not pleased with this false worship. The prophet prophesies the destruction of this temple by Josiah, a descendant of David who will be king of Judah hundreds of years later.

Why is it important to remember that none of us is above God's words of Law and Gospel?

## The Prophet's Disobedience (13:11–34)

The prophet from Judah is deceived by an old prophet from Israel. He disobeys God's command to not go back and eat or drink in Israel.

**CLEAR THE CONFUSION**

**Why did God kill the prophet from Judah?**

The prophet from Judah should have held fast to God's word instead of believing a message someone else claimed to have received from God. The fact that the lion neither mauled nor ate the body of the prophet shows the prophet's death was not the accidental result of a hungry lion hunting prey.

## Prophecy Against Jeroboam (14:1–18)

When Jeroboam's young son becomes ill, Jeroboam sends his wife in disguise to Ahijah, the prophet who had announced Jeroboam would rule over ten tribes. Ahijah prophesies the future of Israel and Jeroboam's house.

## The Death of Jeroboam (14:19–20)

After reigning twenty-two years and conducting wars against Judah, Jeroboam dies. His son Nadab succeeds him as king of Israel.

# Kings of Israel and Judah and the Prophet Elijah (14:21–22:53)

This last section traces the rulers of Israel and Judah. David's descendants in the south have both good and evil kings. All of the kings in the north are evil, continuing in Jeroboam's sins. Finally, God raises up the mighty prophet Elijah to call the Northern Kingdom to repentance.

## Rehoboam Reigns in Judah (14:21–31)

In Judah, Rehoboam continues the idolatry his father, Solomon, introduced through his foreign wives. Five years into Rehoboam's reign, God brings in the king of Egypt to plunder all the treasures Solomon had accumulated in Jerusalem.

## Abijam Reigns in Judah (15:1–8)

Rehoboam's son Abijam rules for just three years. Like his father, Abijam is not wholeheartedly devoted to the Lord. But God is merciful for David's sake and allows David's dynasty to continue ruling Judah. There is frequent warfare between Abijam and Jeroboam, the king of Israel.

**CLEAR THE CONFUSION**

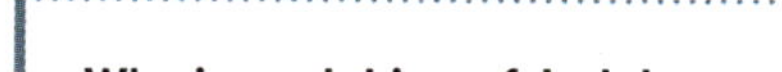

**Why is each king of Judah compared to David?**

David was wholly devoted to the Lord, except in the case of Bathsheba. Even then, David confessed his sin, and God forgave him. God's promise that the Messiah would come from David's line also drove this comparison. It is as if the writer is asking, Is this new son, this new king, the promised Messiah?

What person do you measure yourself against? Which of his or her qualities are you trying to emulate?

## Asa Reigns in Judah (15:9–24)

Asa is favorably compared to King David. He removes the idols from Judah and deposes his wicked mother, who had influenced the two previous kings to seek evil. But the people continue worshiping at the high places instead of coming to be served by God at the temple.

## Nadab Reigns in Israel (15:25–32)

In the northern kingdom, Nadab, Jeroboam's son, is evil like his father. His reign lasts only two years before he is assassinated and Jeroboam's whole family is destroyed. This makes God's mercy on the line of David remarkable, especially after Solomon's wholesale fall into idolatry.

### CLEAR THE CONFUSION

**Was God responsible for the assassination of Nadab and the murder of Jeroboam's whole house?**

No. God prophesied the destruction of Jeroboam's house in 14:10, but Jeroboam was the one responsible for building the two counterfeit temples. 1 Kings 16:7 will show God also held Baasha responsible for murdering Jeroboam's entire house. Baasha did so to secure his own kingship, not to honor God.

## Baasha Reigns in Israel (15:33–16:7)

Baasha, from the tribe of Issachar, starts the second dynasty in Israel. He has a golden opportunity to destroy Jeroboam's two temples, but he does not. God pronounces that his household will be totally wiped out even as he had wiped out all of Jeroboam's house.

What are some natural times in life when you can turn over a new leaf and change your life? How is every worship service just such an occasion?

## Elah Reigns in Israel (16:8–14)

Elah, Baasha's son, rules only two years before he is assassinated by Zimri, a prominent chariot commander. Zimri goes on to cut off all of Baasha's family, as the prophet Jehu had predicted to Baasha. The second dynasty of Israel, Baasha's line, is cut off early in the second generation.

## Zimri Reigns in Israel (16:15–20)

Zimri's self-proclaimed reign lasts seven days. When Israel's soldiers crown their commander Omri king over Israel, he besieges Zimri's fortified city of Tirzah. When Zimri sees the city is taken, he burns himself to death in the king's house.

## Omri Reigns in Israel (16:21–28)

After five years of civil war, Omri begins the third dynasty of Israel. He moves the capital from Tirzah to Samaria and brings order and economic prosperity to Israel. But Omri is an evil king, continuing in the sin of Jeroboam with the two golden-calf temples.

Spouses and friends have such a deep influence on us, often more than we are willing to admit. Think about how you have been influenced by the people that have been close to you in your life. Why is it so important to have Christian friends?

## Ahab Reigns in Israel (16:29–34)

Ahab succeeds his father, Omri, as king. Not only does he continue in Jeroboam's sin, he enters a political marriage with evil Jezebel, the daughter of the king of Sidon. Jezebel spurs him to become the most evil king in the Northern Kingdom's history.

### CLEAR THE CONFUSION

**Why is Hiel of Bethel mentioned (16:34)?**

God had intended Jericho to remain a pile of rubble, a lasting monument every generation of Israelites could visit and remember God's work there. To dissuade any Israelite from rebuilding the city, God pronounced a curse in Joshua 6:26. Hiel paid this steep price for flagrantly disobeying God's will.

### SET THE SCENE

**The Ministry of Elijah the Prophet**

While Israel was being misled by its most evil king, God graciously provided one of Israel's greatest prophets to call His people back to Him. Elijah and his successor, Elisha, would stand out as miracle-working prophets, similar to Moses, who went before them, and Jesus the Christ, who followed them.

## Elijah Predicts a Drought (17:1–7)

God sends Elijah to appear before King Ahab and prophesy a prolonged drought, which will only end at Elijah's word. God then directs Elijah to go and hide himself from Ahab's wrath in a remote area. There, God feeds him in a miraculous way.

### CLEAR THE CONFUSION

**How strong was Elijah's faith?**

As we follow Elijah's story and read the books of the prophets, we will see that all of them struggled from time to time, just as we do. They faced moments of doubt and fear and were deeply affected by the prophecies God sent them to proclaim and by the enemies Satan raised up against them.

## The Widow of Zarephath (17:8–16)

When the brook dries up, God tells Elijah to leave Israel and stay with a widow in Sidon. When Elijah arrives, this poor, destitute woman is preparing a last meal for her son and herself.

## Elijah Raises the Widow's Son (17:17–24)

When the widow's son dies, she accuses Elijah of coming to her to expose her sin and cause her son to die. Elijah struggles with his role as the prophet who brings calamity to everyone to whom God sends him.

Think of some spiritual crises you have faced in your life. How did God lead you closer to Him through them?

### LINK BETWEEN THE TESTAMENTS

**Jesus Mentions Elijah and the Widow's Son (1 Kings 17 → Luke 4:16–30)**

Jesus compares the rejection of His hometown Nazareth to the way the Israelites rejected Elijah. He points out that there were many widows in Israel in Elijah's day, but God only sent His prophet to a non-Israelite living in Sidon.

## Elijah Confronts Ahab (18:1–19)

In the third year of the drought, God commands Elijah to present himself to Ahab and confront him. Elijah proposes a contest between Baal and the Lord.

### SET THE SCENE

**Faithful People in Faithless Times: Obadiah**

While wicked Jezebel was trying to murder all the prophets of the Lord, Ahab's servant Obadiah risked his life to protect one hundred prophets, hiding them in a cave and providing them food and water. He is a reminder that God preserves the faith of His people, even if only a small remnant believe.

## The Prophets of Baal Defeated (18:20–40)

### WAYPOINT

***What does this text show us?***
Elijah challenges the priests of Baal to a contest on Mount Carmel. They slaughter a bull, put it on an altar, and call on their god to send flames to devour the sacrifice without success. Elijah does the same, only he drenches the Lord's sacrifice with water before God consumes it along with the altar.

***What does this text reveal about God's plan of salvation?***
The Holy Trinity—Father, Son, and Holy Spirit—is the only true God. All other gods are the inventions of humans or demons parading as gods. God the Father sent His Son, Jesus Christ, to save us from our sins. He worked great miracles proving He is the Son of God and died on the cross to remove our sins.

People in Elijah's day put their trust in false gods like Baal. In what falsehoods do people put their trust today?

We rarely see great miracles like the people saw in the days of Elijah and Jesus. What impact does reading these miracles have on your faith and confidence in God?

***What does this text uncover about our identity and calling as God's people today?***

Like Elijah, we may well find ourselves surrounded and outnumbered by unbelievers. But we need not fear them. Like the people of Israel and even the prophets of Baal, Satan and his demons have blinded them to the truth. God works through us to tell them about Jesus Christ and His great salvation.

### CLEAR THE CONFUSION

**Wasn't it wrong for Elijah to murder all the prophets of Baal?**

Elijah obeyed God's will in Deuteronomy 13:1–5 when he killed all the prophets of Baal. When Elijah killed the prophets of Baal, he was doing what King Ahab should have done: obeying God's Word to protect the people of Israel.

## The LORD Sends Rain (18:41–46)

Now that Baal worship has been removed from Israel, Elijah humbly prays for God to send rain. Six times, he sends his servant to look for signs of rain, and six times the servant reports that he sees nothing. As Elijah persists in prayer, he sends his servant a seventh time.

## Elijah Flees Jezebel (19:1–8)

Despite God's amazing miracles, Jezebel threatens to murder Elijah instead of showing any repentance. Elijah is crushed, defeated, and crestfallen. Gripped with fear, he flees to the south.

### CLEAR THE CONFUSION

Describe a time you felt totally defeated and discouraged in your faith.

**After seeing God's miracles, how could Elijah be afraid and depressed?**

Elijah considered himself a total failure, fled from his call in Israel, left his servant behind, and went out into the wilderness to die. We need to pray for and encourage our pastors and other commissioned ministers who struggle with the same doubts, fears, and depression, especially when they face rejection.

## The LORD Speaks to Elijah (19:9–18)

In great mercy and patience, the Lord asks Elijah what he is doing way down south on Mount Sinai. Elijah claims to be the last prophet of the Lord. God appears in an unexpected way to reassure and restore Elijah.

## The Call of Elisha (19:19–21)

At God's direction, Elijah enters a field where Elisha is plowing for his father. Elijah lays his cloak over Elisha's shoulders, calling him to follow as a prophet. Elisha holds a solemn feast and then leaves everything to follow after Elijah.

### LINK BETWEEN THE TESTAMENTS

**Elijah Calls Elisha → Jesus Calls His Disciples (1 Kings 19:19–21 → Matthew 4:18–22; 9:9–13)**

After Elijah put his mantle over Elisha's shoulders, Elisha prepared a banquet then left everything to follow Elijah. When Jesus called Peter, Andrew, James, and John, they immediately left their nets and followed Him. When Jesus called Matthew, he prepared a farewell banquet, then left everything to follow Jesus.

## Ahab's Wars with Syria (20:1–12)

The king of Syria lays siege to Samaria. King Ahab meets his first demand, but Ben-hadad has no intention of surrendering to Ahab. Ahab is cut off from his army and surrounded by bureaucrats who fled Ben-hadad's invasion and sheltered behind Samaria's walls.

What is amazing about God protecting Ahab and Israel? What reasurrance does this give you?

## Ahab Defeats Ben-hadad (20:13–25)

An unnamed prophet promises God will deliver Israel from the Syrians with a small detachment of Israelite bureaucrats so that Ahab will have no doubt the Lord is the only true God. Convinced Israel's God only commands the hills, Ben-hadad, the Syrian king, returns the next spring.

### CLEAR THE CONFUSION

**What did the Syrians mean when they talked about "gods of the hills" and "gods of the plains"?**

Ancient peoples believed there were many gods and goddesses with differing degrees of strength and different regions where they could overpower other gods. The Syrians recognized the Lord, Yahweh, as a mighty god. But they thought His power was confined to the hills.

## Ahab Defeats Ben-hadad Again (20:26–34)

The following spring, the Syrians return and vastly outnumber Israel's tiny army. A man of God promises Ahab that the Lord will hallow His name, that is, protect His reputation in the coming battle.

## A Prophet Condemns Ben-hadad's Release (20:35–43)

When God's Word convicts you of sin, how do you normally react: in sullen bitterness or humble repentance? If the former, how can considering the difference between David and Ahab lead you toward repentance and faith?

A son of the prophets confronts Ahab for releasing Ben-hadad instead of executing him as God required. He goes to great lengths to disguise himself and show Ahab his guilt through God's eyes, just as Nathan had once done for David (2 Samuel 12:1–14).

### CLEAR THE CONFUSION

**Why would God kill a son of the prophets for refusing to strike and injure his companion?**

This son of the prophets was disobeying an urgent command of God. God wanted the first man to have a convincing injury so Ahab would really consider the parable he told him. By refusing to obey, this son of the prophets jeopardized God's plan, and his disobedience resulted in his immediate death.

## Naboth's Vineyard (21:1–16)

Because of his ambitious plans for his palace grounds, Ahab covets the vineyard of Naboth. Naboth rightly refuses to sell the land his ancestors received from the Lord. When Jezebel sees Ahab pouting she takes matters into her own hands.

### PICTURE OF THE SAVIOR

**Officials Seek False Witnesses**

Jezebel used false witnesses to accuse innocent Naboth of a capital crime which led to the men of the city stoning him to death. The Jewish high priest Caiaphas sought false witnesses against Jesus in Matthew 26:59.

## The LORD Condemns Ahab (21:17–24)

Elijah confronts Ahab while he is taking possession of Naboth's vineyard. He declares that the kingdom will be snatched away from Ahab and his father's house will be completely exterminated, like the houses of Jeroboam and Baasha. He also prophesies Jezebel's demise.

## Ahab's Repentance (21:25–29)

When confronted by God's powerful Law, Ahab repents. We are left to wonder how different Ahab might have been if he had married a godly Israelite woman instead of Jezebel. Because of Ahab's repentance, God promises to delay the destruction of his house for two more generations.

## Ahab and the False Prophets (22:1–12)

Three years after Naboth's murder, Ahab asks Judah's King Jehoshaphat to fight alongside him against the king of Syria. Jehoshaphat agrees. Not trusting Ahab's false prophets who all promise victory, Jehoshaphat requests to hear from Micaiah, the prophet of the Lord.

## Micaiah Prophesies Against Ahab (22:13–28)

Micaiah warns Ahab his prophets are lying when they promise victory. He describes a scene in heaven that shows a spirit is deceiving him. Ahab refuses to listen to the word of the Lord that would have spared his life.

## Ahab Killed in Battle (22:29–40)

Trying to thwart God's prophecy, Ahab convinces Jehoshaphat to wear his royal robes to the battle while he dresses as a common soldier. But a random arrow proves God's word cannot be broken or outsmarted.

Like Achan (see Joshua 7), Ahab thought he could hide himself from God's judgment among the thousands of Israelite soldiers. How do these two accounts warn us against the sense of anonymity the internet gives when we use it to break any of God's commandments?

## Jehoshaphat Reigns in Judah (22:41–50)

In Judah, Jehoshaphat takes the throne of David. He honors the Lord but displeases God by his alliance with wicked Ahab. Even worse, he seals that alliance by a political marriage between his son Jehoram and Ahab's wicked daughter Athaliah, which will end in near disaster.

## Ahaziah Reigns in Israel (22:51–53)

The book of 1 Kings closes with the beginning of the rule of Ahab's wicked son Ahaziah. Ahaziah follows in the unfaithful footsteps of his father, Ahab, continuing to lead Israel further from the Lord their God.

# 2 KINGS

## Welcome to 2 Kings

What are your first impressions of 2 Kings? What are some specific things you'd like to learn more about?

In the Hebrew Bible, the books of 1 and 2 Kings were together in one scroll. Thus, 2 Kings is a continuation of 1 Kings, which began with King Solomon and ended in the ministry of the prophet Elijah during King Ahab's reign. This second book begins with the close of Elijah's prophetic career, runs through the destruction of the Northern Kingdom, and ends with the destruction of the Southern Kingdom as the people of Judah and Jerusalem are taken into exile in Babylon.

As you read through 2 Kings, watch for God's great patience in sending prophets and faithful kings to lead His people to repentance and faith. Their message is just as valid in our day as it was in theirs. God calls each of us to bring our sin and guilt to Jesus and lay them on Him to carry to the cross.

## 2 Kings at a Glance

- **Start:** The book of 2 Kings begins with the end of Elijah's ministry.
- **End:** 2 Kings concludes with Jerusalem's destruction and the release of the king of Judah from prison in Babylon.
- **Theme:** 2 Kings shows God's great mercy and patience in the midst of His judgment against the idolatry in Israel and Judah.
- **Author and Date:** The author of 2 Kings is unknown. It was likely composed around 560 BC.
- **Places Visited:** Jerusalem and Samaria
- **Journey Time:** The twenty-five chapters of 2 Kings can be read in approximately two and a half hours.
- **Outline:**
  - Jehoram's Reign in Israel and the Prophet Elisha (1:1–8:15)
  - Kings of Israel and Judah Until Israel's Defeat and Captivity (8:16–17:41)
  - Judah's Last Kings (18:1–24:20)
  - Judah's Fall and Exile (25:1–30)

# Five Top Sights and Spectacles of 2 Kings

**Elijah Taken Up to Heaven (2:1–14)** Watch God take the prophet up to heaven without experiencing death.

**The Ministry and Miracles of Elisha (2:1–7:20)** See the double portion of the Spirit at work in the prophet.

**The Near Extinction of David's Line (11:1–21)** Follow Joash's escape from the dangerous palace to the safety of God's temple.

**The Destruction and Exile of Israel (17:1–41)** See the captives of Israel led in chains from Samaria to Assyria.

**The Destruction of the Temple and Exile to Babylon (25:1–21)** Watch as the remnant of Jerusalem is dragged out of the Promised Land to captivity in Babylon.

# Seeing Jesus in 2 Kings

We see Jesus most clearly in how He shared the rejection and mistreatment of His prophets and in the destruction of the temple, which Jesus references when He later says, "Destroy this temple, and in three days I will raise it up" (John 2:19). Just as Solomon's temple was destroyed then rebuilt after Israel's "burial" in Babylon, Jesus would be put to death on the cross, buried in a tomb, and raised in glory on the third day.

# Jehoram's Reign in Israel and the Prophet Elisha (1:1–8:15)

In this section, Elijah denounces Ahab's son Ahaziah for his wickedness. Elijah is taken up to heaven, and Elisha succeeds him as prophet to the Northern Kingdom of Israel. Then, we read eight accounts from Elisha's ministry.

Where do your friends seek advice when they face challenges in life? Where do you tend to turn for help?

## Elijah Denounces Ahaziah (1:1–18)

After Ahaziah falls through the lattice work covering a window, he sends messengers to asks Baal if he will recover. God sends Elijah to intercept them and tell Ahaziah he will die for not consulting the God of Israel.

### CLEAR THE CONFUSION

**Why did God destroy the first two companies of soldiers but spare the third (1:9–16)?**

King Ahaziah sent large squads of soldiers to intimidate Elijah. The commanders of the first two companies mocked Elijah when they called him "man of God." But the third commander humbled himself before Elijah, honoring the prophet and begging him to spare his life and the lives of his men.

## Elijah Taken to Heaven (2:1–14)

### WAYPOINT

***What does this text show us?***
As Elijah walks with Elisha, they are separated by horses and chariots of fire, and Elijah is taken up into heaven by a whirlwind without experiencing death.

***What does this text reveal about God's plan of salvation?***
Not all believers will experience death. Those who are alive when Jesus returns to judge the world will instantly be transformed to live in God's presence forever.

***What does this text uncover about our identity and calling as God's people today?***
We can look forward with joy and confidence to the life we will enjoy with God because of Jesus' perfect salvation. God calls us to share His Law and Gospel with others that they, too, may turn from their sin and look forward to the eternal life Jesus Christ has won through His life, death, and resurrection.

What do you think are some reasons God chose to bring Elijah to heaven without him dying first?

When Jesus returns, would you prefer to be alive or raised from the dead? Why?

Elijah's departure in the whirlwind reminds us of the day Jesus Christ will return to judge the living and the dead and to restore His creation. How does the knowledge of His coming change the way you think about a situation that is troubling you today?

### CLEAR THE CONFUSION

**What is the double portion of the spirit that Elijah promised to Elisha?**

In the days of the Old Testament, the Holy Spirit was present in all believers to create and sustain their faith. But a special measure of the Holy Spirit was given to kings, priests, and prophets to fulfill their work. When Elijah left, Elisha knew he needed the Holy Spirit to carry on the work of two prophets.

Elisha's cursing of the youth gang seems harsh, but they were unrepentant and trying to silence God's word. What are some harsh situations that you have seen bring people to repentance?

## Elisha Succeeds Elijah (2:15–25)

When the sons of the prophets see Elisha use Elijah's rolled-up mantle to part the Jordan River, they know God has raised him up to succeed Elijah. He further proves this by healing the foul water from a spring and dealing with a gang of youth who were mocking and threatening him.

**PICTURE OF THE SAVIOR**

**Mockery**

The Israelites showed their deep disdain for the Lord and His prophets by mocking and taunting Elijah and Elisha. Jesus suffered the same mockery and taunting on the cross but instead of calling down fire from heaven or cursing them, Jesus prayed for His Father to forgive them (Luke 23:34).

## Moab Rebels Against Israel (3:1–27)

After Ahab dies, the Moabite king rebels and withholds his tribute payment. Jehoram marches out with Judah and Edom to subdue them. When the three armies run out of water, Elisha promises that God will provide water and hand the king of Moab over to the alliance.

**CLEAR THE CONFUSION**

**Why did wrath come against Israel when Moab's king sacrificed his son?**

The Moabite king sacrificed his heir to win the sympathy of his god Chemosh. This shows Jehoram's demands were overly cruel or he refused to accept Moab's terms of surrender and wanted to slaughter the Moabites. Israel's two allies withdrew, and that withdrawal ended Jehoram's campaign.

## Elisha and the Widow's Oil (4:1–7)

The history of Israel's kings is set aside to record eight accounts from the ministry of Elisha. In this first account, God miraculously provides for a widow of one of the sons of the prophets through Elisha. This prevents her two sons from being sold into slavery to pay her late husband's debts.

## Elisha and the Shunammite Woman (4:8–17)

A wealthy woman from Shunem builds a rooftop chamber for Elisha to stay in whenever he passes through. Elisha promises her she will give birth to a son within a year, and she does.

## Elisha Raises the Shunammite's Son (4:18–37)

When the Shunammite's son suddenly dies, she quickly travels to Mount Carmel to summon Elisha. He sends his servant Gehazi ahead to lay his staff on the child's face. Elisha arrives with the woman and raises her son.

Every resurrection account in the Old and New Testaments reminds us of the day Jesus rose from the dead and the Last Day when He will raise all the dead. What comfort, reassurance, and encouragement do you find in these resurrection accounts?

**PICTURE OF THE SAVIOR**

**Elisha and Jesus Raise Dead Children**

Just as the Shunammite woman rushed to Elisha to get help for her son, Jairus the synagogue ruler rushed to Jesus. Like Elisha, Jesus raised the child from the dead. Unlike Elisha, however, who prayed to God to raise the child, Jesus, the Son of God, merely said, "Little girl, I say to you, arise" (Mark 5:41).

## Elisha Purifies the Deadly Stew (4:38–44)

We see two miracles in this passage. Through Elisha, God purifies a large pot of stew that the sons of the prophets can't afford to throw away during a famine. Then, through Elisha, God multiplies twenty loaves of barley and fresh ears of grain to feed a hundred men.

Through Elijah's and Elisha's ministries, we frequently see God caring for the physical and material needs of His people. Jesus showed the same through His healing miracles. Why do we need to be reminded that God cares about our material and physical needs as well as those of our soul?

**PICTURE OF THE SAVIOR**

**Miraculous Feedings**

Under Elisha, God's word multiplies a little bread to feed one hundred men. Twice, the Gospels record Jesus miraculously feeding much larger crowds. Miracles proved that Elijah and Elisha were genuine prophets of the Lord. But the might and vast number of Jesus' miracles proved Him to be God's own Son.

## Naaman Healed of Leprosy (5:1–14)

***What does this text show us?***

Elisha directs Naaman, a Syrian commander with leprosy, to wash seven times in the Jordan. Though Naaman initially refuses, servants convince him to submit to God's word.

Why do you think Naaman was so furious at Elisha's directions?

How would you convince a stubborn friend to do something you know would be good for them, but they don't see it?

Big moments of God's deliverance are rare in this life. Why is it more important to look for the simple but always present means of grace God gives to strengthen our faith?

Leprosy was a powerful visualization of the devastating effect sin has on us. How does Naaman's cleansing give us a glimpse of Baptism's power?

***What does this text reveal about God's plan of salvation?***

God brings us His salvation through simple means—His Word, Baptism, and Holy Communion. The Spirit creates faith through these means, not mighty miracles.

***What does this text uncover about our identity and calling as God's people today?***

God's children believe His promises in simple faith by the Holy Spirit's power. God calls us to trust the Spirit working through His Word of Law and Gospel, which we also share with others that the Spirit might convict them of their sins and give them saving faith.

## Gehazi's Greed and Punishment (5:15–27)

When Naaman is healed, he brings a huge reward to Elisha, which the prophet declines. Gehazi, Elisha's servant, helps himself to a small portion of it. Elisha tells Gehazi he was there in spirit and saw everything Gehazi did. As punishment, Gehazi is afflicted with Naaman's leprosy.

### CLEAR THE CONFUSION

**Why did Elisha refuse Naaman's gift?**

God wanted Naaman to understand His forgiveness and healing are completely free gifts of His grace and love; they cannot be earned by sinful humans. When Gehazi asked for a portion of that reward, he could have given Naaman the impression that his gift was part of the reason God had healed him.

A lost axe head seems rather insignificant when we think of the bigger challenges Elisha faced. Think of a problem that vexes you but feels pretty insignificant to bring to God's attention. How does God's concern for this son of the prophets encourage you to bring every concern to God in prayer, no matter how insignificant it may seem?

## The Axe Head Recovered (6:1–7)

As Elisha accompanies the sons of the prophets to the Jordan to cut wood to enlarge the building, a borrowed axe head falls into the river. In mercy, God uses a stick Elisha throws into the water to make the iron float so the man can retrieve it and not have to purchase a new one.

## Horses and Chariots of Fire (6:8–23)

When the king of Syria learns that Elisha has been alerting the king of Israel to ambushes he has set, he sends a large Syrian army to capture Elisha. God uses two miracles involving sight and blindness to encourage Elisha's servant and protect Elisha and Israel from their enemies.

## Ben-hadad's Siege of Samaria (6:24–33)

The Syrian king again comes and lays siege to Samaria. When Samaria's food supply runs out, it leads to cannibalism between two Israelite women. The horrified king of Israel sends a messenger to execute Elisha, likely because he had counseled the king not to surrender but to instead trust God.

### SET THE SCENE

**Ancient Sieges**

To capture fortified cities, invading armies surrounded the city, cutting off any help that could come from neighboring cities, as well as food from its fields, vineyards, and pastures. Sieges frequently lasted years. Even undesirable items like donkeys' heads and dove manure became highly coveted food.

### CLEAR THE CONFUSION

**Why would God force this mother to eat her child?**

God didn't. Elisha had promised the Lord would rescue Samaria and they only needed to trust Him and wait patiently. She did not trust God and took matters into her own hands. The truly tragic thing is that the woman only needed to wait one more day, when God miraculously lifted the siege.

Sarah lost patience waiting for a son. Saul lost patience waiting for Samuel when he saw his army melting away. This woman lost patience in God and killed her own child. Name a situation that is really trying your patience and tempting you to take matters into your own hands.

## Elisha Promises Food (7:1–2)

Elisha promises that the next day the Samaritans will be able to buy seven quarts of fine flour for a single shekel, when today it costs eighty shekels to buy a donkey's head. When a high official expresses skepticism, Elisha says he will see this but never eat the food.

The Israelite official's skepticism is understandable. Elisha had promised what seemed impossible—though the Syrian camp held all the food the people of Samaria needed. Think of a situation in your life that once seemed impossible. How did God resolve that situation?

## The Syrians Flee (7:3–20)

Four starving Samaritan lepers go out to surrender to the Syrians and discover the Syrians have fled, leaving behind all their supplies of food and provisions. When the lepers share the news in Samaria, the people rush out into the fields and find Elisha's prophecy fulfilled.

## The Shunammite's Land Restored (8:1–6)

Elisha had previously warned the Shunammite woman (from 2 Kings 4) to flee a coming seven-year famine. Afterward, when she returns to the king to ask for her house and property, Elisha's servant is recounting to the king how God had raised her son from the dead.

## Hazael Murders Ben-hadad (8:7–15)

Ben-hadad, king of Syria, sends his servant Hazael with an enormous gift to inquire of Elisha if he will recover from his illness. When Elisha tells Hazael he will be king of Syria, Hazael murders Ben-hadad.

**PICTURE OF THE SAVIOR**

**Elisha Weeps**

Elisha wept over the needless pain unrepentant Israel would soon bring upon itself. We see that same pain and grief in Jesus when He wept over Jerusalem, prophesying its destruction and the deep sufferings the Jews would bring upon themselves by rejecting Him, their promised Savior (see Luke 19:41).

# Kings of Israel and Judah Until Israel's Defeat and Captivity (8:16–17:41)

Having completed the eight incidents from Elisha's ministry, this section traces the course of Israel and Judah from Elisha's death to the destruction of the Northern Kingdom, Israel, because of their idolatry and unfaithfulness.

## Jehoram Reigns in Judah (8:16–24)

In Judah, Jehoram, the son of godly Jehoshaphat, is influenced by Athaliah, his wicked wife and Ahab's daughter. He does great evil in the sight of the Lord, which is recorded in 2 Chronicles. His reign only lasts eight years.

## Ahaziah Reigns in Judah (8:25–29)

Ahaziah, the son of Jehoram and Athaliah, rules in Judah after his father's death. He is an evil king, deeply influenced by his mother Athaliah. His reign will be cut off after one year when he goes to visit his uncle, Israel's King Joram.

Jehoshaphat of Judah was a good and faithful king, but his alliance with Ahab brought Athaliah into his family. It didn't turn Jehoshaphat himself away from God, but it did result in the unbelief of his son and grandson and the near extinction of his line. Which of your friendships and relationships do you think could deeply harm your family?

## Jehu Anointed King of Israel (9:1–13)

Elisha sends a servant to a military commander named Jehu, who is holding a war council against Syria. In Elisha's name, the servant separates Jehu from the other commanders, anoints him Israel's king, and commissions him to destroy the entire house of Ahab.

## Jehu Assassinates Joram and Ahaziah (9:14–29)

Israel's King Joram (Ahab's grandson) is recuperating from a battle wound in Jezreel, his capital. Jehu leads a company of commanders toward Jezreel to destroy the household of Ahab.

**SET THE SCENE**

**God's Justice: Naboth Vindicated**

In 1 Kings 21, Jezebel had the elders stone Naboth so Ahab could seize his vineyard. Here in 2 Kings 9:26, we learn Naboth was not the only one killed in Jezebel's plot; his sons were murdered as well because they were the rightful heirs of that property. Here God vindicates this faithful believer and his family.

Jezebel, Ahab's wicked wife, was personally responsible for murdering many faithful prophets in her goal to replace the prophets of the Lord with her Baal prophets. Though she prospered unopposed for so many decades, God finally punished her. Though all sinners will face God's righteous judgment on the Last Day, why is it important that sinners are sometimes punished in this lifetime?

## Jehu Executes Jezebel (9:30–37)

After fulfilling God's will by destroying Joram and Ahaziah, Jehu rides into Jezreel. When Jezebel appears at the window, defiantly decked out in her queenly finery, eunuchs cast her out the window at Jehu's word, and she is trampled to death by horses and her body eaten by dogs.

## Jehu Slaughters Ahab's Descendants (10:1–17)

Jehu obeys God's word by slaughtering Ahab's seventy sons. Then he goes beyond God's word by murdering Ahab's relatives, great men, and close friends in Jezreel as well as the relatives of Judah's King Ahaziah. Jehu will be called to account for this self-serving bloodshed (see Hosea 1:4).

## Jehu Strikes Down the Prophets of Baal (10:18–27)

Jehu separates the Baal worshipers from the worshipers of the Lord and strikes down the Baal worshipers as well as his prophets. Jehu targets these Baal worshipers not because he is zealous for the Lord but because they were associated with the house of Ahab.

## Jehu Reigns in Israel (10:28–36)

Because Jehu destroys the house of Ahab as God had decreed, the Lord promises his family will rule Israel until the fourth generation. Nevertheless, Jehu continues in the sins of Jeroboam, Israel's first king who had built the golden calves in the north and south of his kingdom.

## Athaliah Reigns in Judah (11:1–3)

**VISUALIZE**

After Jehu assassinates her son Ahaziah, Athaliah, Ahab's wicked daughter, seizes the throne of Judah for herself and tries to destroy the royal house of Judah, David's house, in order to secure her throne.

## Joash Anointed King in Judah (11:4–20)

**WAYPOINT**

***What does this text show us?***
Seven years into Athaliah's reign, the priest Jehoiada organizes two divisions of Levites to isolate Athaliah from her supporters and defend Joash (also called Jehoash), sole-survivor from the line of David. They anoint Joash as king and seize Athaliah.

***What does this text reveal about God's plan of salvation?***
Through Athaliah, Satan tried to break God's plan to send His Son from the line of David. The devil tried again when Jesus was a young child and King Herod sought to exterminate the child he feared would take his throne.

***What does this text uncover about our identity and calling as God's people today?***
God has made us His children through Holy Baptism and guards us by His Spirit through God's Word and Sacraments. He saves His church from Satan's plots and continues to guard and preserve us from all harm and danger.

Athaliah felt the Levites committed treason when they deposed her. How can God's Word guard you from being so deceived by sin that you think God is wrong and you are right?

What comfort do you draw from God repeatedly foiling Satan's attempts to cut Jesus off?

How is it a comfort to know you don't need to uncover every plot against you because God has it in hand?

## Jehoash Reigns in Judah (11:21–12:3)

Jehoash begins ruling Judah as a young boy. He is faithful to the Lord as long as the priest Jehoiada is alive to influence him. But the people of Judah cling to their high places rather than single-mindedly seeking God in Solomon's temple.

## Jehoash Repairs the Temple (12:4–18)

During the reigns of wicked Jehoram, Ahaziah, and Athaliah, Solomon's temple was neglected and fell into disrepair. Young Jehoash directs Jehoiada and the priests to make repairs.

## The Death of Joash (12:19–21)

The book of 2 Kings records the assassination of Judah's King Joash (Jehoash) by two of his servants. In 2 Chronicles 24, we learn that after Jehoiada the priest died, Joash abandoned the Lord and put to death Jehoiada's son who called him to repent and return to the Lord his God.

Jehoahaz repented and turned to God when he fell into difficulties, but he didn't commit his reign to God by removing Jeroboam's golden calves. What sinful desire do you find most difficult to set aside to serve God and your neighbor?

## Jehoahaz Reigns in Israel (13:1–9)

In the Northern Kingdom of Israel, Jehoahaz, Jehu's son, reigns and continues in the sins of Jeroboam, worshiping in the houses of the two golden calves. To call him to repentance, God gives Israel into the hands of Hazael, king of Syria, and Hazael's son, Ben-hadad.

## Jehoash Reigns in Israel (13:10–13)

After Jehoahaz dies, the third generation of Jehu's family takes the throne in the person of Jehoash. Like his father and grandfather, Jehoash does not return to Ahab's Baal worship but clings to the two golden calves of Jeroboam. He is known for his successful wars against Judah.

## The Death of Elisha (13:14–25)

When Israel's King Joash (Jehoash) learns Elisha is dying, he comes to him lamenting. Elisha directs him to shoot arrows to be assured God will give him victory over the Syrians. God performs a miracle through Elisha's dead body.

## Amaziah Reigns in Judah (14:1–22)

Amaziah becomes king of Judah after his father, Joash, is assassinated (2 Kings 12:21). Amaziah does not actively turn to other gods, but he is not wholeheartedly devoted to the Lord and His temple as David was. He becomes proud after defeating Edom and is humbled by Israel.

When Israel enjoyed peace and prosperity, it quickly forgot about God and chased after idols. How easily do you find yourself forgetting to thank and serve God when He gives you times of peace and prosperity? Why might it be advantageous for you to undergo difficult times when God permits them?

## Jeroboam II Reigns in Israel (14:23–29)

God is gracious during the long reign of Israel's new king, Jeroboam II. With Syria and Assyria weakened, Jeroboam is able to extend his northern borders back to where they had been in Solomon's time. But Israel's material prosperity makes them wander further from the Lord.

### SET THE SCENE

**Which prophets did God send to Jeroboam II?**

When Elisha died, Israel saw the last of its great, long-serving prophets. But God still raised up prophets for the nation of Israel. During the lifetime of Jeroboam II, God sent Amos and Hosea. In the books of these prophets, you will see God's amazing patience and love for His people.

## Azariah Reigns in Judah (15:1–7)

Azariah (also called Uzziah later in this chapter and in 2 Chronicles) enjoys one of the longest reigns of Judah's kings. Like his father before him, Azariah is faithful to the Lord yet does not remove the high places. Azariah is struck with leprosy and his son becomes coruler.

## Zechariah Reigns in Israel (15:8–12)

The last king from the line of Jehu is Zechariah, his great-great-grandson. After six months he is assassinated, ending Jehu's dynasty in Israel. The next twenty-two years are a time of great instability and turmoil during which Israel will be ruled by five kings, three of whom will be assassinated.

In Martin Luther's explanation of "daily bread" in the Fourth Petition of the Lord's Prayer, he includes "devout and faithful rulers" and "good government." Thinking back through your life, what difference has resulted from good and bad government leaders? How can this turbulent instability in Israel's rulers remind us how important it is for us to continually pray for officials in our government?

## Shallum Reigns in Israel (15:13–16)

Shallum reigns only a month before he is assassinated by a conspirator named Menahem. Menahem reveals his cruel and godless character in the atrocities he inflicts on the city of Tirzah when it refuses to cooperate with his conspiracy. He tries to destroy the next generation of Tirzah.

## Menahem Reigns in Israel (15:17–22)

When the Assyrians demand tribute from Israel, Menahem takes it from the people of Israel rather than from his own wealth. The prosperity the people had enjoyed under Jeroboam II is gone, and within a generation, Israel will cease to exist as a nation.

**SET THE SCENE**

**The Assyrians**

The Assyrians menaced the entire Near East. They crushed and deported Israel in 722 BC, and almost did the same to Judah not long after. Only the direct hand of God stopped Judah from being massacred and deported during the time of Hezekiah. The Assyrian empire was later conquered by Babylon.

## Pekahiah Reigns in Israel (15:23–26)

Menahem's son Pekahiah only reigns two years before pressure from Assyria causes his military leaders to rise up in a coup against him. Pekahiah is killed by his captain, Pekah, who takes the throne after him.

## Pekah Reigns in Israel (15:27–31)

Pekah reigns over Israel for twenty years before he is assassinated. Assyria begins to whittle down the territory of Israel again, taking the land east of the Jordan River and, in the north, the land where Jesus will grow up and conduct His Galilean ministry.

Consider how the political instability caused by assassinations and the loss of land through foreign invasion affected the people of Israel. Why do you think so few turned to God in repentance?

## Jotham Reigns in Judah (15:32–38)

In Judah, after his father, Azariah (Uzziah), is struck with leprosy, Jotham begins to reign. He is a good king but makes no effort to remove the high places and center Judah's worship on the temple. God begins sending Israel and Syria against Judah to bring the people to repentance and faith.

## Ahaz Reigns in Judah (16:1–20)

Ahaz arises as one of Judah's most evil kings, even sacrificing his own son. When pressured by Israel and Syria, Ahaz allies himself with the Assyrians. He even replaces the temple's bronze altar with a copy of a foreign altar.

**PICTURE OF THE SAVIOR**

**The Virgin Shall Conceive**

One of the most famous messianic prophecies arose while Ahaz was out in a field wondering how to save Judah from Israel and Syria. Isaiah assured the king God would protect Judah. When Ahaz refused to request a sign, the Lord Himself gave Ahaz the sign—"the virgin shall conceive" (Isaiah 7:14).

## Hoshea Reigns in Israel (17:1–5)

Israel now has its last king. In an attempt to hold off Assyrian invasion, Hoshea pays annual tribute. But when he reaches out to Egypt for help and stops paying tribute, the Assyrian king sweeps through the Northern Kingdom and lays siege to Samaria, the capital, for three years.

## The Fall of Israel (17:6)

### VISUALIZE

In the third year of the siege, Samaria collapses. The Assyrian king captures the surviving Israelites and carries them off into exile. These ten tribes lose their national identity and are never restored to their land. They are known as the "ten lost tribes." They are a warning to us that though we have been redeemed by the blood of Christ, the Passover Lamb, if we reject Christ and stubbornly forsake Him, we will lose the inheritance He won for us.

## Exile Because of Idolatry (17:7–23)

### WAYPOINT

***What does this text show us?***

The thankless people of Israel refused to obey and serve God. God graciously and persistently sent prophets to call them back to Him, but the people refused. They even sacrificed their children to idols and committed all kinds of other atrocities. Finally, God drove them out of His sight.

***What does this text reveal about God's plan of salvation?***

God is merciful, gracious, and patient. He sent His prophets to the people of old. He sent His Son to suffer and die in our place, saving the world. He sent His apostles to declare His mercy and grace through His Word. But there will be a day of judgment when those who reject Him will be cast off forever.

***What does this text uncover about our identity and calling as God's people today?***

Today is the day for us to recognize that we have the same sinful inclination to reject God and to follow our own desires and the temptations of Satan and the world around us. Christ calls us to repent, trust in Him, and enjoy forever the inheritance He is preparing for us.

How did Israel's identity as children of Abraham and the people of God give them false confidence they could sin without any consequences?

What things in Jesus' life and public ministry show us God's patience and long-suffering?

Why is it important to ask God to expose and root out the sins that have such a hold over us, even those that seem so insignificant to us?

### Assyria Resettles Samaria (17:24–41)

The Assyrians break the identity of nations they conquer by exiling them and scattering them throughout other regions they have conquered. For this reason, the Israelites are removed from their land, and Gentiles from various eastern regions are brought in to be settled in their place.

**SET THE SCENE**

**The Samaritans**

The hostility between Judeans and Samaritans began when Israel was divided into two kingdoms and frequent wars erupted. The Assyrians resettling Gentiles into Samaria increased this hostility. In Ezra we will see this enmity increase again when the Samaritans oppose the rebuilding of the temple.

## Judah's Last Kings (18:1–24:20)

This section covers the time from the destruction of the Northern Kingdom, Israel, to the fall of the Southern Kingdom, Judah, and its exile in Babylon. Two faithful kings rule in Judah, Hezekiah and Josiah. The rest are very wicked.

### Hezekiah Reigns in Judah (18:1–12)

God raises up Hezekiah, one of Judah's most faithful kings and comparable to David himself. Hezekiah removes the high places and all the objects of idolatry throughout Judah. He reestablishes the temple worship and trusts God enough to break his father's alliance with Assyria.

Pull up a map of your state and imagine every city and town being captured by an enemy nation, which has now turned its attention against your own city. Describe a situation in your life that seemed as hopeless as the situation Hezekiah faced when the Assyrian army surrounded Jerusalem. What comfort does God's Word give you for such times?

**CLEAR THE CONFUSION**

**Was Hezekiah wrong to break Moses' bronze serpent to pieces (18:4)?**

This was among the list of actions Hezekiah took to restore proper worship in Judah. The people of Judah had taken that object, which turned repentant people to faith in God in the wilderness (Numbers 21:4–9), and made a false god out of it. Sadly, it needed to be destroyed.

### Sennacherib Attacks Judah (18:13–37)

Sennacherib, the Assyrian king, invades Judah and captures every fortified city but Jerusalem. Sennacherib sends his commander in chief to discourage the people of Jerusalem from trusting Hezekiah and to convince them to surrender. In the process, he blasphemes God.

## Isaiah Reassures Hezekiah (19:1–7)

Hezekiah knows he is powerless to oppose Sennacherib. He sends priests to the prophet Isaiah. Isaiah assures Hezekiah that God has heard Sennacherib's insulting words and promises He will use a report to drive away, then defeat, the Assyrian king.

## Sennacherib Defies the LORD (19:8–13)

The Lord keeps His promise through a rumor that comes to the Assyrian king concerning an army from Cush (near Egypt in north Africa) coming to fight against him. Sennacherib withdraws from his siege but sends messengers with a letter that again blasphemes God.

## Hezekiah's Prayer (19:14–19)

Hezekiah is not relieved by the withdrawal of the Assyrian forces. He carries the message to the temple and unfolds it before God's eyes. He prays for God to hallow His name and show other nations that He is the only true God by rescuing Jerusalem from the Assyrians.

## Isaiah Prophesies Sennacherib's Fall (19:20–37)

God reveals His answer to Hezekiah through a message by the prophet Isaiah. It mocks Sennacherib and exposes his foolish sin. The Lord sends His angel who destroys 185,000 Assyrian soldiers in one night. Sennacherib withdraws his army to Assyria.

### PICTURE OF THE SAVIOR

**The Lord Sends His Angel to Defend His People**

One angel killed 185,000 Assyrian soldiers in one night.

When Jesus was arrested, He told Peter, "Do you think that I cannot appeal to My Father, and He will at once send Me more than twelve legions of angels?" (Matthew 26:53).

When He returns on Judgment Day, He will return as the glorious Lord of the angel armies and will send them to gather all people to Himself for judgment.

In Matthew 18:10, Jesus states that every believing child has a guardian angel. In Luther's Morning Prayer and Evening Prayer, we ask God to send His holy angel. What comfort does this give you when you think of one angel driving away the overwhelming army of the Assyrian Empire?

## Hezekiah's Illness and Recovery (20:1–11)

While Jerusalem is besieged by the Assyrians, Hezekiah becomes very ill. Isaiah tells him to set his house in order because he will not recover. Hezekiah humbles himself and fervently prays for healing. God sends Isaiah to return and tell him God hears him and will heal the disease and give him fifteen more years. God works a miracle with the sun's shadow to reassure Hezekiah that He will fulfill His promise.

### CLEAR THE CONFUSION

**Can we change God's mind through our prayers?**

That is the wrong question. In most situations, we don't know God's will, so we can't know if He has changed His mind or not. What we do know is that God commands us to pray and invites us to lay our concerns before Him.

## Hezekiah and the Babylonian Envoys (20:12–21)

When the king of Babylon learns God has cured Hezekiah's illness, he sends an envoy with presents to congratulate him. In pride, Hezekiah shows off his storehouses of wealth. Isaiah confronts him for his pride and for relying on his wealth and his alliance with Babylon against Assyria.

### SET THE SCENE

**What was the conduit that brought water into the city (20:20)?**

While the Assyrian army was approaching Jerusalem, Hezekiah channeled the water from the Gihon Spring outside Jerusalem into the Pool of Siloam inside the city's walls. Hezekiah's engineers tunneled through more than 1,700 feet of solid rock. This tunnel was discovered in 1838 and can be seen to this day.

As no king had done since David, Hezekiah removed all places of idol worship and restored the temple to its rightful place as the only place to worship God. But very quickly his son Manasseh restored that false worship and plunged Judah into grievous evil. How can regular, weekly worship help us avoid the power of sin to enslave us?

## Manasseh Reigns in Judah (21:1–9)

Manasseh, Hezekiah's son, has one of Judah's longest reigns at fifty-five years but  is the most evil of all David's descendants. He quickly undoes all the good things his father, Hezekiah, had done. He restores the high places, sacrifices his son as a burnt offering, and leads Judah to evil.

## Manasseh's Idolatry Denounced (21:10–18)

Manasseh's sins are so great and Judah has become so evil that God is no longer willing to spare David's kingdom. Because of Manasseh, Judah is now doomed to destruction and exile like Israel before it.

## Amon Reigns in Judah (21:19–26)

Amon, Manasseh's son, is just as wicked as his father. After only two years, his servants conspire and put him to death. But the people of Jerusalem do not permit these servants to seize the throne. They keep an heir of David on the throne, making eight-year-old Josiah their king.

## Josiah Reigns in Judah (22:1–2)

Hezekiah's great-grandson Josiah follows in his faithful footsteps, doing what is right in God's eyes faithfully—just as David had done. This is the last king of Judah who receives such praise for his faithfulness.

## Josiah Repairs the Temple (22:3–7)

In the eighteenth year of his reign, Josiah orders the priests to repair the temple, which again has fallen into disrepair through the unfaithfulness of Manasseh and Amon.

## Hilkiah Finds the Book of the Law (22:8–20)

While cleaning the temple, the high priest finds the Book of the Law, which Moses had written. When it is read to Josiah, he is filled with fear and tears his garments because of the sins of his father and grandfather, which stirred God's wrath against Jerusalem. When he sends the priests to consult a prophetess, he learns that Jerusalem and Judah are condemned to destruction. But because Josiah is repentant, he is assured the destruction and captivity will not come during his lifetime.

When Hezekiah knew the destruction from the Babylonians would not happen in his lifetime, he did not let it concern him. Josiah was quite different. He set out to reform Judah, even destroying one of Jeroboam's golden-calf temples. What are some things you can seek to do in your congregation to make a positive impact for future generations?

## Josiah's Reforms (23:1–20)

Josiah removes all objects of false worship from Judah and even from portions of Israel. He goes to one of Jeroboam's golden-calf temples and desecrates the altar. This fulfills the word the man of God had prophesied to Jeroboam in 1 Kings 13:2.

## Josiah Restores the Passover (23:21–27)

Josiah restores the celebration of the Passover. His celebration exceeds that of Hezekiah and all the kings before him. But despite Josiah's faithfulness God is still determined to destroy Judah and Jerusalem, implying that most of the people of Judah are not as sincere and repentant as Josiah.

## Josiah's Death in Battle (23:28–30)

When Josiah learns the king of Egypt is marching his army past Israel to engage the Assyrians, he involves himself in the conflict and is mortally wounded in battle. He is the last faithful king of Judah. He will be succeeded by a string of four evil kings—three of his sons and his grandson.

## Jehoahaz's Reign and Captivity (23:31–35)

After Josiah's death, the people of Judah make his second son, Jehoahaz, king. Jehoahaz is an evil king who rules only three months before the king of Egypt deposes and imprisons him. He dies in Egypt. Pharaoh replaces him with his older brother, Eliakim, whom he renames Jehoiakim.

## Jehoiakim Reigns in Judah (23:36–24:7)

Jehoiakim is an evil king like his brother Jehoahaz. He rules eleven years, during which the Babylonian king Nebuchadnezzar defeats the Egyptians in the Battle at Carchemish. He makes Jehoiakim his servant, or vassal. After serving Babylon for three years, Jehoiakim rebels.

## Jehoiachin Reigns in Judah (24:8–9)

Jehoiakim is succeeded by his son, Josiah's grandson, Jehoiachin. Like his father and his uncles, he does evil in the sight of God.

### Jerusalem Captured (24:10–17)

VISUALIZE

When Nebuchadnezzar's army came to lay siege to Jerusalem, Jehoiachin surrendered himself and the city. He was taken captive and exiled to Babylon along with his family and everyone of military age. The temple and the king's palace were looted and their wealth carried off to Babylon. Among the exiles was the prophet Ezekiel. Nebuchadnezzar left behind the poor and untrained so they would not rebel against him. He also made Jehoiachin's uncle Zedekiah, Josiah's third son, a vassal king of Judah.

In Jeremiah 24 and 29, God speaks very favorably about King Jehoiachin and all the exiles who voluntarily surrendered to Nebuchadnezzar the king of Babylon and were taken into exile. God promised to be with them and restore them to Jerusalem. What confidence can this give you when you face a new phase of life?

### Zedekiah Reigns in Judah (24:18–20)

Zedekiah, Judah's last king, reigns eleven years and does evil in Jerusalem. He, too, rebels against the king of Babylon. We learn more about him in the book of Jeremiah (see chapters 34, 37–38).

## Judah's Fall and Exile (25:1–30)

This section describes the fall of Judah and how the Babylonians took Judah's survivors into exile. It ends with the elevation of Judah's King Jehoiachin from prison to the table of the Babylonian king.

### Fall and Captivity of Judah (25:1–21)

WAYPOINT

***What does this text show us?***

Zedekiah rebels against Babylon, and Nebuchadnezzar lays siege to Jerusalem. When the city wall falls, Zedekiah tries to flee but is captured, blinded, and taken into exile. The temple, the king's house, and all the great houses are burned to the ground, and the walls around Jerusalem are all broken down.

Zedekiah could have reigned in peace as a vassal king to Babylon, but he lost it all when he rebelled. How is his life a warning when we are tempted to rebel against God our King?

Describe a time when your life was shattered and you felt helpless. How did God guide you through that time?

Recall a time you gathered with other Christians beyond your congregation. What comfort do you find in remembering Christ's Church stretches around the world?

***What does this text reveal about God's plan of salvation?***

The exile does not threaten God's plan of salvation—it is more like a seventy-year detour until God brings His people back to Jerusalem to rebuild the temple and prepare for Christ's arrival. In the meantime, God raises up prophets for His surviving people—Jeremiah, Ezekiel, and Daniel.

***What does this text uncover about our identity and calling as God's people today?***

Believers in Jesus Christ are spread throughout the world, living as if in exile while we await the day our Savior will return to gather us together from the ends of the earth. Meanwhile, wherever God has placed us, we glorify His name by sharing the Good News of Jesus Christ and serving our neighbor.

## SET THE SCENE

**Where can I read about the temple being rebuilt and the walls restored?**

The book of Ezra records the rebuilding of the temple. The book of Nehemiah narrates the rebuilding of Jerusalem's walls. Both rebuildings took place in the midst of great danger and opposition, chiefly from the Samaritans.

## Gedaliah Made Governor of Judah (25:22–26)

Though the vast majority of Judah is dead or in exile, Nebuchadnezzar leaves the poorest of the poor to tend the vineyards and fields to keep them productive. Over this tiny remnant, he appoints Gedaliah as governor, and Jeremiah the prophet remains with them.

## Jehoiachin Released from Prison (25:27–30)

### VISUALIZE

The book of 2 Kings ends with a glimmer of hope as Josiah's grandson, King Jehoiachin, who was imprisoned in exile for thirty-seven years, is suddenly freed by a new emperor who has taken the throne. Jehoiachin eats at Evil-merodach's table in an honored place above the other kings at his table. He receives this honor and a regular allowance for the remainder of his life.

A little over halfway through the seventy-year exile the prophet Jeremiah had foretold, King Jehoiachin was released from prison. What impact do you think that made for the Judean exiles? Think of an unexpected favor you received. How might that encourage your trust in God's care and providence?

### CLEAR THE CONFUSION

**What is so significant about this ending of 2 Kings?**

After thirty-seven years, the exiles may have felt God had forsaken and forgotten them and they would never return. But Jehoiachin's release showed them God had not forgotten His people. More importantly, Jehoiachin's release meant the line of David continued toward Jesus Christ.

# 1 CHRONICLES

## Welcome to 1 Chronicles

The two books of Chronicles made up one scroll in the Old Testament Scriptures. In the Hebrew Bible, they were the very last scroll, written to encourage the exiles who had returned to rebuild the temple in Jerusalem after seventy years of exile in Babylon and who were facing fierce opposition from the Samaritans and other enemies.

The book of 1 Chronicles focuses on God raising up David to make preparations for the temple his son will build and David organizing the priests and Levites who will bring God's gifts to Israel in that temple throughout the generations until the Messiah Himself comes. As you read this book, you will find the same encouragement and inspiration as you receive Christ's gifts in worship and wait patiently for His second coming.

What do you know about 1 Chronicles? Do any narratives or images come to your mind when you reflect on this book? What are some specific things you'd like to learn more about?

## 1 Chronicles at a Glance

- **Start:** 1 Chronicles begins with a genealogy retracing the generations from Genesis through 1 Samuel.
- **End:** 1 Chronicles concludes with David making preparations for the temple Solomon will build.
- **Theme:** 1 Chronicles shows God raising David to bring peace to Israel and organize the worship that would center in God's temple.
- **Author and Date:** The author of 1 Chronicles is unknown, but many Bible scholars think Ezra wrote it. It was likely composed around 430 BC.
- **Places Visited:** Jerusalem, Gibeon, Mount Gilboa, Hebron, Ammon, Syria, Zion
- **Journey Time:** The twenty-nine chapters of 1 Chronicles can be read in approximately two hours.
- **Outline:**
  - Nations and Israel in God's Plan of Salvation (1:1–9:34)
  - The Establishment of David's Reign and the Centrality of the Ark of the Covenant (9:35–17:27)

The first nine chapters of 1 Chronicles are genealogical lists, similar to many family trees in which some people are known while others' lives are a mystery. What do you know of your family tree? How can you show your gratitude to God for the ancestors who came before you?

- David's Military Campaigns (18:1–20:8)
- David Prepares for Location and Building of the Temple (21:1–22:19)
- David Organizes Temple Worship (23:1–26:32)
- David Leaves the Kingdom to Solomon (27:1–29:30)

## Five Top Sights and Spectacles of 1 Chronicles

**David Anointed King (11:1–3)** Watch the tribes of Israel come to make David their king.

**David Takes Jerusalem (11:4–9)** See David conquer the fortified city and make it his own capital.

**The Ark Brought to Jerusalem (15:1–29)** Follow David when he dances before the ark as it is carried into Jerusalem.

**David Charges Solomon to Build the Temple (22:6–19)** Listen as David encourages Solomon to carefully follow God's design for building the temple.

**David Organizes the Priests and Levites (23:1–24:31)** Watch David establish the order of priests and Levites, who will bring God's gifts to His people in the temple up until Jesus' time.

## Seeing Jesus in 1 Chronicles

The first place we see Jesus is the genealogies that start 1 Chronicles. Chapter 1 contains the line from Adam to Jacob, chapter 2 takes us from Jacob to David, and chapter 3 traces the descendants of David, which is the line from which Jesus received His human nature. Many names from these lines will be found in Matthew 1 and Luke 3.

Two events in 1 Chronicles also point to Jesus. The first is when David brings the ark of the covenant into Jerusalem in chapter 15. The ark is brought up with large crowds, singing, and great celebration, just as Jesus was carried into the city on the foal of a donkey to the praises of the crowds in Jerusalem on Palm Sunday.

The second event is God's promise to David, "I declare to you that the Lord will build you a house" (17:10). This is the promise that the Messiah, or Christ, will be a descendant of David.

### What to Do with Genealogical Lists

The long genealogical lists that make up the first nine chapters of 1 Chronicles can be very intimidating. You might find it helpful to skim over the names and focus on the headings and the narrative mixed in with the names. *Guiding Word* will set the context for you and help you draw some meaning out of these lists.

## Nations and Israel in God's Plan of Salvation (1:1–9:34)

Through genealogies, the Chronicler retraces the descendants of Adam and Eve through Abraham, David, and the exiles who have returned from Babylon.

### From Adam to Abraham (1:1–27)

These names span the time from creation through Noah's flood to God's call for Abraham. After Noah, the list broadens to show us that all nations now living on the earth had their origin in Noah's three sons, Shem, Ham, and Japheth.

Notable descendants of Ham include the Egyptians (v. 8); Nimrod, who founded Assyria and Babylon (v. 10); and Canaan (vv. 13–16), whose descendants became the wicked nations Israel conquered under Joshua. Our Savior's line continues from Noah's son Shem to Abraham in verses 17–27.

### From Abraham to Jacob (1:28–54)

We now turn to Abraham's descendants. After listing Abraham's sons and grandchildren through Hagar, a concubine, and Keturah, the wife he took after Sarah died, we see Isaac, the son God had promised to Abraham and Sarah.

The Chronicler next leads us through Esau's many descendants, because these people of Edom had much interaction with the returned exiles.

### A Genealogy of David (2:1–55)

Chapters 2 through 9 focus on the descendants of Jacob, the twelve tribes of Israel. Three particular tribes—Judah, Levi, and Benjamin—receive the most attention because these were the three tribes in the Southern Kingdom of Judah. These also made up most of the returned exiles to whom the Chronicles were written.

God changed Abram's name to *Abraham* to indicate he would be the father of all believers, both Israelites and Gentiles. That means all believers are children of Adam, Noah, and Abraham. How can the example of these three believers encourage you to trust God's salvation in Jesus Christ and serve Him faithfully and boldly?

Jacob's genealogy begins with Judah because that is the tribe from which came David and his son Solomon, the two primary figures in the books of Chronicles. It is also the tribe of the leaders of the returned exiles, and the coming Savior.

An important verse in this passage mentions Achan, "the troubler . . . who broke faith" (2:7) by stealing items from Jericho that were reserved for the Lord (see Joshua 7). These same Hebrew words will be used in 2 Chronicles of the unfaithful kings who bring trouble on Judah and lead to the Babylonian captivity.

Another prominent person in this passage is Bezalel (v. 20). He was the skilled designer and builder of the tabernacle on Mount Sinai in the days of Moses (see Exodus 31). He also made the bronze altar before which Solomon prays for wisdom in the first chapter of 2 Chronicles. Throughout the Chronicles, we will notice how the kings and the temple, which held the furnishings built by Bezalel, are intertwined.

David is held up as Israel's greatest king, yet he fell far short of God's Law. What enabled David to keep going forward and serving God after committing such terrible sins?

The frailty and flaws of David and his descendants remind us that our salvation rests completely upon Jesus' perfect life, death, and resurrection. How does Jesus' complete salvation set you free to serve God and your neighbor?

What do you know about the dark chapters in your family's history? How does Jesus' forgiveness give you a new start?

## Descendants of David (3:1–24)

**WAYPOINT**

***What does this text show us?***

Chapter 3 unfolds the messianic line through David's son Solomon beginning in verse 10. These names will appear in depth in 2 Chronicles as the flawed kings of Judah.

***What does this text reveal about God's plan of salvation?***

King David and his descendants were sinners in need of the Messiah, Jesus Christ. Jesus' holiness and perfection did not come from His ancestors but from being the only-begotten Son of God the Father. The flawed human ancestors of Jesus remind us that Jesus came to save all sinners.

***What does this text uncover about our identity and calling as God's people today?***

Every one of us is a sinner washed clean by the blood of Jesus Christ, our perfect Savior. God has cleansed us—like King David and his descendants—of all our sins and has called us to serve Him by serving our neighbors and declaring His praises.

## Descendants of Judah (4:1–23)

This section of the genealogies gives us a broader view of the tribe of Judah beyond David and his descendants. It includes the so-called Prayer of Jabez found in 4:9–10.

## CLEAR THE CONFUSION

**The Prayer of Jabez**

Some writers take this obscure passage out of context and claim that if you really want something, just lay claim to it in prayer and God will grant that prayer. But the Chronicler included this prayer to encourage the returned exiles to pray for God to deliver them from enemies who sought their annihilation.

Think of a time of great distress in your life. How did that distress affect the urgency in your prayers to God? How did God answer those prayers and deliver you from that distress?

## Descendants of Simeon (4:24–43)

The descendants of Simeon are listed next. Like Levi, this tribe had been scattered among the other tribes. They maintained their tribal identity as Simeonites but lived peaceably within the borders of Judah and are among the exiles who have returned.

## Descendants of Reuben (5:1–10)

We turn to the two and a half tribes that settled east of the Jordan River in Gilead (see Joshua 1:12–18; 22:1–34). These tribes were successful when they were allied with Judah and fell into captivity when they were not. He appeals to the exiles of Reuben to ally themselves with Judah once again.

## Descendants of Gad (5:11–22)

Gad had cried out to God in battle, and "He granted their urgent plea because they trusted in Him" (v. 20). This is powerful encouragement to the exiles who were surrounded by deadly enemies. They, too, should cry out to God, trusting Him to grant their urgent plea.

## The Half-Tribe of Manasseh (5:23–26)

The history of the eastern half-tribe of Manasseh reminds the returned exiles of the danger of returning to idolatry. God had given them great success, just like Manasseh's earlier victories in battle. But if they abandon the Lord, He will once again give them into the hands of their enemies.

What was the benefit of God choosing a single tribe and a single family within that tribe to be the priests and spiritual leaders in Israel until the Messiah came?

What were the shortcomings of sinners being the spiritual leaders in Israel? How does Jesus' perpetual high priesthood benefit the members of His New Testament Church?

Washed in Jesus' blood in our Baptism, we have been cleansed to offer our lives as living sacrifices to our Lord. What are some of the ways you serve the Lord in your daily life?

## Descendants of Levi (6:1–81)

WAYPOINT

***What does this text show us?***

The descendants of Levi include Moses and Aaron, Israel's first high priest. Aaron's family became the priests of Israel. The Levites assisted the priests and were spread throughout the land of Israel to teach the Israelites God's ways.

***What does this text reveal about God's plan of salvation?***

This genealogy shows the work of Aaron's priesthood was never complete, because a new high priest had to be anointed each generation. It points to the need of a greater priest—Jesus Christ, who offered Himself as our sacrifice once for all and intercedes as our great High Priest at the Father's right hand.

***What does this text uncover about our identity and calling as God's people today?***

Just as He had done with the Levites, God has spread us among the nations to teach our families, friends, and neighbors about God's forgiveness and salvation in Jesus Christ.

## Descendants of Issachar (7:1–5)

The Chronicler turns to the other tribes of Israel. The descendants of Issachar had very humble beginnings, yet by the time of David, they had multiplied into a mighty force. Though the returned exiles are few in number, God will also multiply them.

CLEAR THE CONFUSION

**Where is Dan?**

The Chronicler does not mention the tribe of Dan. The most likely reason is because they hadn't trust God enough to undertake the difficult task of driving out the stubborn Canaanites from their allotted land. They captured a different, easier land and quickly turned to idolatry (see Judges 18).

Similarly, the exiles were finding it difficult to rebuild Jerusalem with their stubborn enemies. They may have been tempted to abandon the struggle to rebuild the temple. We also need the same faith and trust in Jesus Christ, when life becomes difficult, lest our names be blotted out of the Book of Life.

The disappearance of Dan from 1 Chronicles and Revelation is puzzling. But when you trace their story in Judges 18, you learn that they were not content with the inheritance God gave them through Joshua. They took their own land and established their own worship and priesthood. How is Dan's disappearance from the Scriptures an important reminder to keep Christ Jesus first in your life?

## Descendants of Benjamin (7:6–12)

At the close of Judges, Benjamin was the smallest tribe and nearly exterminated. Yet they were the tribe from which Israel's first king, Saul, came. Likewise, the exiles were few in number but important to God and safe in His hand.

## Descendants of Naphtali (7:13)

Naphtali was Israel's sixth son by Rachel's maidservant, Bilhah. No mention is made of warriors from this tribe.

## Descendants of Manasseh (7:14–19)

This is the other half-tribe, located in Canaan west of the Jordan River. Verse 15 mentions the daughters of Zelophehad, whose question for Moses led to a provision for passing down a man's inheritance when he left daughters but no sons (Numbers 27:1–11; 36:1–12).

## Descendants of Ephraim (7:20–29)

Ephraim was the chief tribe of the northern kingdom, Israel. This passage relates how Ephraim's children were killed in a raid by Philistines. Ephraim's wife bears him another son, named Beriah, ancestor of Joshua, Moses' aide, who led Israel into the Promised Land.

Perhaps it seems strange that this personal tragedy that struck Joseph's son is recorded in 1 Chronicles and not in Genesis. While Israel was in Egypt, Ephraim's children were killed in a raid. His brothers comforted him. Who has comforted you when you suffered loss and grief? How can you comfort others who are struck with such loss and grief?

## Descendants of Asher (7:30–40)

The last tribe mentioned is Asher, which had a large number of mighty warriors. Despite their military strength, they were exiled because they turned from God. Again, this is a reminder to the exiles to trust in God's power to accomplish His purposes even when they became numerous.

## A Genealogy of Saul (8:1–40)

We next turn to the tribe of David's predecessor, Israel's first king, Saul. Unfaithful King Saul is only mentioned in passing, along with his three sons (v. 33). The line continues through the descendants of Jonathan, faithful Israelite and close friend of David.

## A Genealogy of the Returned Exiles (9:1–34)

Before moving on to David's kingship, the Chronicler lists the Israelites who returned from exile in Babylon. This genealogy reminds the exiles that God has graciously made them a continuation of the nation of Israel.

# The Establishment of David's Reign and the Centrality of the Ark of the Covenant (9:35–17:27)

The Chronicler explains how God gave David the throne over all Israel after the death of King Saul. He establishes his reign and has the ark of the covenant brought into Jerusalem, his new capital city.

## Saul's Genealogy Repeated (9:35–44)

The Chronicler now prepares to transition to the main theme of 1 Chronicles: God establishing the reign of David and his house. He presents one final genealogy, the genealogy of Saul—both his ancestors and his descendants through his son Jonathan, David's dear friend.

## The Death of Saul and His Sons (10:1–14)

**VISUALIZE**

The Chronicler recounts only one event from Saul's reign: his disgraceful death. Rather than cry out to God in his distress, Saul takes his own life. The Chronicler ascribes Saul's death to his breaking of faith with God (v. 13)—a sin we will see frequently among the Davidic kings in 2 Chronicles and among the people of Judah, which would lead to exile in Babylon. But just as God restored Israel's kingship by raising David to the throne, so He restored the exiles to the land He had promised to Abraham, Isaac, and Jacob.

## David Anointed King (11:1–3)

The remainder of 1 Chronicles covers the same ground as 2 Samuel. The elders of Israel recognize that David had led the army of Israel under King Saul in former days, so they go to Hebron to make him king.

## David Takes Jerusalem (11:4–9)

David captures Jerusalem from the boastful Jebusites. In reading how God helped David, the exiles are encouraged to face their defiant neighbors. Just as David raised Jerusalem from the rubble of war, God will help them, too, raise it from the rubble of its Babylonian destruction.

## David's Mighty Men (11:10–47)

Next is a list of the prominent soldiers who joined forces with David while Saul was seeking his life. The three mighty men at the top of the list are more valiant than all David's other fighting men. Conspicuously absent from the list of thirty is Joab, commander of David's armies.

## The Mighty Men Join David (12:1–40)

More groups of soldiers join David while he is living among the Philistines in Ziklag as a fugitive from Saul. These include kinsmen of King Saul from Benjamin who defect to join David. Later, vast numbers of Saul's troops come to Hebron to proclaim David king.

## The Ark Brought from Kiriath-Jearim (13:1–4)

David wishes to restore Israel's spiritual health, which King Saul had so sorely neglected. He gathers the priests and Levites to bring the ark of the covenant up to Jerusalem. The exiles did something similar. They built the altar before laying the temple foundation to offer sacrifices.

## Uzzah and the Ark (13:5–14)

**VISUALIZE**

In 1 Samuel 6–7, we learned how the ark came to be in Kiriath-jearim in the house of Abinadab. Forty years later, David brings it up to Jerusalem on a cart. When the oxen stumble and the ark starts to totter, Uzzah reaches out to steady it, and God strikes him down. Fearful that God is opposed to the moving of the ark, David stops the procession, and the ark remains at the home of Obed-edom. During the three months it remains there, God richly blesses that household, indicating to David that the ark will bring blessings if handled correctly.

What comfort do you think the exiles took from remembering that David had lived in exile just like them and that God had raised him up and returned him to Israel? What difference does it make for you to know Jesus Christ will return, restore creation, and bring us to His eternal kingdom?

This steady parade of soldiers leaving Saul's army to pledge their allegiance to King David is similar to the church militant, Christ's church on earth. Every day, people from every tribe, people group, nation, and language are called from Satan's kingdom and given faith in Jesus Christ through Word and Sacrament. Many face great persecution to do so, but the Holy Spirit strengthens and encourages them. How might this account have encouraged the small group of exiles trying to rebuild Jerusalem? How does it encourage you when the enemies of Christ seem so powerful and numerous?

Where is God's mercy and grace for Uzzah? Uzzah's sin was not unforgivable, but it did have earthly consequences. God's holiness is important, and it is important for us to realize God has established a way for sinners like us to approach Him and receive forgiveness, which is through Jesus Christ alone. How can this account of Uzzah's death remind us to revere and treasure the body and blood of our Savior in Holy Communion?

**CLEAR THE CONFUSION**

**Why did God strike down Uzzah for keeping the ark from falling?**

Uzzah had the best intentions, but he violated God's word. The ark represented God's throne among His people. Even the high priest could not touch it. He could only approach it in the Most Holy Place one day each year to sprinkle blood on it. The ark was meant to be carried by its poles by Levites.

## David's Wives and Children (14:1–7)

Perhaps still reeling from the incident with the ark, several concurrent events convince David that God favors him and has established him as king. A foreign king generously offers to build his house from the famous forests of Lebanon. David's family grows dramatically.

**CLEAR THE CONFUSION**

**Was God pleased with David taking more wives?**

David's polygamy was against God's original plan for lifelong marriage of one man and one woman. The Old Testament does not explicitly condemn polygamy, but every account of it in the Scriptures reflects rivalry, pain, and suffering.

## Philistines Defeated (14:8–17)

The Philistines learn David is king of Israel and come against him in rage. After inquiring of God, David attacks and wins a great victory. When the Philistines rise up again, God directs him to come around from behind and David routs the Philistines.

The ark was the symbol of God's presence among His people. Though the returned exiles did not have the ark to put in their rebuilt temple, God promised something greater: the Messiah would stand in these temple courts (see Malachi 3:1). What encouragement do you find from Jesus' promise that "where two or three are gathered in My name, there am I among them" (Matthew 18:20)?

## The Ark Brought to Jerusalem (15:1–29)

David studies the Books of Moses to learn the proper way to transport the ark. He carefully organizes the Levites: some will carry the ark, some will serve as guards, and others will play musical instruments to bring up the ark with great rejoicing.

**PICTURE OF THE SAVIOR**

**The Ark of the Covenant Brought into Jerusalem**

When David had the ark brought into Jerusalem, there was a mighty parade, with great joy and celebration. When David's greater Son, Jesus Christ, entered Jerusalem on Palm Sunday, great crowds welcomed Him, shouted, and sang praises.

**CLEAR THE CONFUSION**

**Why did Michal become so angry toward David?**

When Michal saw David humble himself by setting aside his royal robes and wearing the same lowly clothing the priests and Levites wore, she despised him in her pride. As punishment, God closed her womb so she did not bear to David an heir. This completed the separation of Saul's house from David's.

## The Ark Placed in a Tent (16:1–7)

David prepares a tent to house the ark of the covenant. This is not the tent or tabernacle that Moses built in the wilderness. That tent still remains at the high place in Gibeon. Again, notice David's careful selection of Levites to guard the ark and make music before the Lord.

## David's Song of Thanks (16:8–36)

David arranges portions of three psalms for the Levites. David is an important figure in formalizing Israel's worship for generations to come. His many psalms continue to bless God's people until the day Christ returns, perhaps even beyond that great and glorious day!

David's psalms spoke of God's protection of the patriarchs, which he himself received while fleeing from Saul. The returned exiles also knew God's protection. What situation(s) in your life do these psalms address?

## Worship Before the Ark (16:37–43)

**VISUALIZE**

David assigned priests and Levites to worship both before the ark of the covenant in the tent in Jerusalem and before the tent of meeting at the high place in Gibeon—the tabernacle of Moses, where the sacrifices were still being burned upon the bronze altar, which Bezalel built for Moses.

### The LORD's Covenant with David (17:1–15)

When David contemplates building a house for God, the Lord promises to build an eternal house for David, raising one of his descendants to be the Christ. God permits David to make preparations and store up supplies for the temple, but his son Solomon will actually build it.

### David's Prayer (17:16–27)

David humbly praises God for raising him to this position and for His promise to establish the rule of David's house forever by bringing forth the Christ from David's line.

## David's Military Campaigns (18:1–20:8)

The Chronicler describes David's wars with neighboring nations, which won for Israel all the land God had promised Abraham and brought peace to Israel from its enemies on every side.

### David Defeats His Enemies (18:1–13)

God gives David victory over his enemies all around. The Chronicler is careful to note that when David took spoils of war, he set them aside to be used to build the temple and its furnishings.

### David's Administration (18:14–17)

David's impartial justice points ahead to Jesus' justice on Judgment Day. What cases of injustice trouble you? How can remembering Jesus' forgiveness and His perfect judgment comfort you?

David establishes justice in the land, administering the law equitably to everyone in Israel. Having come from a very poor family, David is careful not to show partiality toward the rich or powerful.

### The Ammonites Disgrace David's Men (19:1–9)

David sends ambassadors to the new Ammonite king after his father has died. The new Ammonite king intentionally disgraces David's ambassadors. The Ammonites remain hostile to Israel clear up to the time of Nehemiah, who came to Jerusalem to rebuild the exiles' city walls.

**CLEAR THE CONFUSION**

**Why did the Ammonites shave the Israelite ambassadors' beards and cut off half of their clothes?**

The princes of the Ammonites convinced their new king that David was sending spies to conquer their land. By disgracing David's representatives, the Ammonites forced a war with Israel. To brace for this war, they hired mercenaries from Syria. Meanwhile, David sent his army to answer this disgrace.

### Ammonites and Syrians Defeated (19:10–19)

Outnumbered and surrounded, Joab divides Israel's army and attacks both the Syrian mercenaries and the Ammonites. The Syrians flee and the Ammonites retreat to the fortified city of Rabbah. When the Ammonites summon more Syrians, David leads the army against them.

### The Capture of Rabbah (20:1–3)

Joab leads the attack against the Ammonites, laying siege to Rabbah and capturing it. The Ammonite king's crown is given to David, his wealth is looted, and his people are made servants of the Israelites. This ends the Ammonite rebellion.

We might wonder why the Chronicler wrote such a long, detailed account of this battle with the Ammonites. Possibly it was to encourage the returned exiles not to be intimidated by the powerful Ammonites who were opposing their rebuilding of Jerusalem. When you are surrounded by problems that seem insurmountable, how can this account give you courage to trust in God's deliverance?

### Philistine Giants Killed (20:4–8)

Though David defeated the Philistines in two previous battles, they come against him again in a series of battles. The Chronicler describes three incidents when Philistine giants fall at the hands of individual Israelite soldiers. The exiles need not fear their powerful enemies.

## David Prepares for Location and Building of the Temple (21:1–22:19)

Though God forbids David to build the temple, He reveals to David the future location of the temple and permits him to gather building materials for the temple his son Solomon will build.

## David's Census Brings Pestilence (21:1–17)

What details of this narrative stand out most to you?

How does this account deepen your understanding of the salvation Jesus accomplished for all people on the cross?

Picture the Angel of the Lord holding his sword over your unbelieving family, friends, coworkers, or neighbors. How does that increase your urgency to share Christ's salvation with them?

**WAYPOINT**

***What does this text show us?***

Satan incites David to order a census of his military. In punishment, God sends a plague on Israel. As the Angel of the Lord approaches Jerusalem, God orders Him to sheath His sword. David confesses his sin and asks God to punish him and his father's house.

***What does this text reveal about God's plan of salvation?***

Not far from this place, Jesus, the Son of David, will take that punishment and the punishment for all our sins upon Himself when He suffers and dies on the cross in our place.

***What does this text uncover about our identity and calling as God's people today?***

Like the people of Jerusalem, we deserve death for our sin, but God has graciously given His Son and sheathed the sword of His wrath. Rejoicing in the forgiveness, peace, and restoration Jesus has won for us, we boldly share the good news of His salvation to a world living in sin and darkness.

Altars were important to the people of God throughout the Old Testament. David was directed to build this altar and offer burnt offerings and peace offerings on it. Each altar was a foreshadowing of the cross of Jesus, where He offered Himself as a sacrifice to satisfy God's wrath and free us from His punishment. How does the altar in your church point back to Jesus' sacrifice for the sins of the world?

## David Builds an Altar (21:18–22:1)

God commands David to build an altar at the spot where the Angel of the Lord sheathed his sword. David announces this is where the temple will be built. In this same place, the exiles will rebuild the temple, and near here, Christ will be punished in our place on the cross.

## David Prepares for Temple Building (22:2–5)

David was instrumental in the extensive preparations to build the temple. He organizes the resident aliens to be stonecutters and sets aside huge quantities of building materials.

## Solomon Charged to Build the Temple (22:6–19)

David explains to his son Solomon why God forbade him to build the temple and charges Solomon to build it after David's death. David urges him to carefully observe the statutes God gave Moses. David then commands the leaders of Israel to help Solomon build the temple.

# David Organizes Temple Worship (23:1–26:32)

In preparation for the temple Solomon will build, David organizes the priests and Levites for orderly service in God's house. He establishes a schedule for the service of the priests and Levites as well as the Levite guards and musicians.

## David Organizes the Levites (23:1–32)

The next portion of 1 Chronicles highlights the central importance of the temple and the arrangements David made to formalize the service of the priests and Levites. Some Levites will maintain the house of the Lord; others will be officers, judges, gatekeepers, and musicians.

## David Organizes the Priests (24:1–31)

With the help of two priests, David organizes Israel's priests into twenty-four divisions. David's plan provides uninterrupted service of the priests before the Lord. Each division serves for approximately two weeks each year.

**LINK BETWEEN THE TESTAMENTS**

**Abijah's Division of Priests Serves at the Temple (1 Chronicles 24:10 → Luke 1:5–23)**

When David cast lots for the order of service for the twenty-four divisions of priests, the eighth lot fell to Abijah. One of Abijah's distant descendants would be a priest named Zechariah. While Zechariah's division was serving at the temple, he was chosen by lot to offer incense in the temple. As he was doing that work, the angel Gabriel appeared to him to announce that his wife, Elizabeth, would have a son named John (that is, John the Baptist).

## David Organizes the Musicians (25:1–31)

Next, David organizes the Levite musicians into twenty-four choruses, each serving two weeks per year, like the priests. Each division consists of twelve musicians. David also establishes formal instruction in music so coming generations could continue to honor God with music.

Sacred music in worship was clearly important to David. He set all of his psalms to music, and he arranged for the Levites to pass their musical training from one generation to the next. What does music add to your worship experience?

## Divisions of the Gatekeepers (26:1–19)

The Levite gatekeepers serve as temple guards, protecting the temple and its furnishings and guiding those who come to the temple courts. They will be the key to protecting Joash, the sole surviving member of David's line, from the usurping Athaliah (see 2 Chronicles 23).

The Levites in charge of the treasury were responsible for disbursing funds for building and maintaining the temple. While Aaron's sons had the responsibility of the priesthood, Moses' descendants oversaw the temple treasury. What do you know of the responsibilities of your congregation's treasurer and finance officers?

## Treasurers and Other Officials (26:20–32)

David chooses Moses' offspring to be in charge of the temple finances, which were vast. The treasuries consist of offerings given by the people as well as the plunder of wars and the gifts of Israel's leading generals.

# David Leaves the Kingdom to Solomon (27:1–29:30)

David makes his final preparations to hand the kingdom over to his son Solomon. He arranges a standing army, charges Israel to serve God and assist Solomon in building the temple, and charges Solomon to study and obey God's Word and to build the temple.

## Military Divisions (27:1–15)

In the peace of David's later reign, he organizes a strong standing army, capable of driving out invading nations. Each month, a division of 24,000 men serves under one of David's mighty men. Thus Israelite soldiers in peacetime function as a reserve army.

## Leaders of Tribes (27:16–34)

This passage lists the military leaders of each tribe in Israel. It mentions David's census, which had brought the Lord's anger upon Israel. Next are the overseers of David's property, and the last verses present David's personal advisers, including Ahithophel who betrayed him (2 Samuel 15).

## David's Charge to Israel (28:1–8)

David gathers all his officials and Solomon is publicly anointed as king to succeed David. David charges these officials to be loyal to Solomon, as they have been to him, to assist Solomon in building the temple, and to keep the Law of God.

## David's Charge to Solomon (28:9–21)

David publicly charges Solomon to build the temple, giving him the precise designs for the temple which God had commanded him (see 28:19). David charges Solomon to be faithful to God—to seek God or to be cast off by God forever.

## Offerings for the Temple (29:1–9)

David declares additional freewill offerings he will give toward the temple. His officials freely and joyfully offer more materials for the construction of the temple, which causes great rejoicing among the people and in David's heart.

## David Prays in the Assembly (29:10–22a)

David offers a prayer acknowledging that all the gifts he and the officials have offered for the temple actually first came from God's hands. He prays that God will keep this spirit of faith and love of the Lord in the hearts of Solomon and each Israelite.

## Solomon Anointed King (29:22b–25)

Not only does David proclaim Solomon his successor but the nation of Israel also proclaims Solomon its king. In many ways, the kingdom of Israel grew even more powerful, prosperous, and peaceful in the early years of Solomon's reign.

## The Death of David (29:26–30)

The Chronicler records David's death. Then he mentions several historical annals to prove his writings about David are not acts of fiction but historical fact.

Looking back over his reign, David could have taken great pride in his military victories, the expansion of Israel's territory, and the peaceful conditions toward the close of his reign. He could have taken credit for the temple plans and the large stores of supplies he had contributed. Instead, he publicly reminds all his officials and the people of Israel that God is the source of all he has been able to do as king. Why is it important to keep a similar view toward our possessions and our accomplishments?

### CLEAR THE CONFUSION

**What are the Chronicles of Nathan the prophet and of Gad the seer?**

These are writings of David's prophets that have been lost to time. But there is another possibility. We know the prophet Samuel wrote the first chapters of 1 Samuel, but after his death (1 Samuel 25:1), who wrote the rest? Could the prophets Nathan and Gad have written the remainder of 1 Samuel and all of 2 Samuel? The prominent involvement of both of these priests in the life and reign of David makes this an intriguing possibility.

# 2 CHRONICLES

## Welcome to 2 Chronicles

What do you know about 2 Chronicles? What are some specific things you'd like to learn more about?

The book of 1 Chronicles focused on King David's preparations for his son Solomon to build the temple and his organization of the priests and Levites to bring God's gift to His people in that temple.

Now, 2 Chronicles traces the history of Judah from Solomon building the temple to its destruction by the Babylonians (the time period covered in 1 and 2 Kings). It closes with the proclamation of a Persian king for the Judean exiles to return to Jerusalem and rebuild the temple.

As you read this book, consider how important the temple and God's gifts given there were to each king. Consider what value you place on receiving the gifts Jesus gives at church each week.

## 2 Chronicles at a Glance

- **Start:** 2 Chronicles begins with Solomon worshiping at Gibeon and God granting him discretion and wisdom.
- **End:** 2 Chronicles concludes with the Persian king Cyrus's decree to rebuild God's house in Jerusalem.
- **Theme:** 2 Chronicles shows the centrality of the temple to the spiritual health of Israel and its kings.
- **Author and Date:** The author of 2 Chronicles is unknown, though some Bible scholars believe Ezra wrote it. It was likely composed around 430 BC.
- **Places Visited:** Jerusalem, Gibeon, Ammon, Syria, Zion
- **Journey Time:** The thirty-six chapters of 2 Chronicles can be read in approximately two and a half hours.
- **Outline:**
  - History of Solomon and Building of the Temple (1:1–9:31)
  - Division of the Kingdom of Israel (10:1–12:16)
  - The Davidic Dynasty Before the Assyrian Invasion (13:1–26:23)
  - Invasions and the Fall of the Davidic Dynasty (27:1–36:23)

## Five Top Sights and Spectacles of 2 Chronicles

**Solomon Builds the Temple (3:1–17)** Watch Solomon construct the house of the Lord.

**The Division of the Kingdom (10:1–11:23)** Discover how Rehoboam divides Israel and then strengthens Judah through the temple.

**Jehoshaphat's Unwise Alliance with Wicked Ahab (17:1–22:12)** Trace the path of destruction that results from righteous Jehoshaphat allying his kingdom with wicked King Ahab of Israel.

**God Delivers Hezekiah and Jerusalem (32:1–33)** Watch God's angel deliver Judah from an overwhelming world power.

**Cyrus's Decree (36:22–23)** Listen as God works through a pagan king to free His exiles to rebuild the temple.

The temple and all its furnishings foreshadowed the life and ministry of God's Son, Jesus Christ. Which furnishings in your church most remind you of Jesus' saving work? Why are such visible objects important for us?

## Seeing Jesus in 2 Chronicles

This book focuses on the centrality of the temple which represented God's dwelling with His people. The temple strongly foreshadows the work of Jesus Christ, the mediator between God and mankind. At the same time, the history of the temple's destruction and rebuilding strongly foreshadows Jesus' death and resurrection.

## History of Solomon and Building of the Temple (1:1–9:31)

In this section, Solomon sets his heart on worshiping the Lord. God gives him discretion and great wisdom to rule His people and build the temple. Solomon amazes the queen of Sheba with his wisdom, and his death is recorded.

### Solomon Worships at Gibeon (1:1–6)

Solomon gathers the officials of Israel, and together they seek the Lord at the high place at Gibeon. There at God's altar, Solomon offers a thousand burnt offerings.

### CLEAR THE CONFUSION

**Why did Solomon make his sacrifices at Gibeon instead of Jerusalem?**

Moses' tabernacle and the bronze altar for Israel's offerings were at Gibeon at that time. The ark had been carried out of the tabernacle by Eli's sons in 1 Samuel 4. When the Philistines returned the ark, it was kept in Kiriath-jearim instead of being returned to the tabernacle. Finally David brought it up to Jerusalem and placed it in a tent. Solomon gathered the leaders of Israel in Gibeon before the tabernacle to seek God's help and blessing before building the temple.

## Solomon Prays for Wisdom (1:7–13)

During the night, God invites Solomon to request whatever he wishes. Solomon requests discretion and knowledge to lead God's people. Pleased with Solomon's prayer, God gives him riches, possessions, and honor greater than any king before or after.

Solomon's prayer was remarkable. Like David, his father, he was most concerned with ruling for the good of his people. In humility, he confessed his youth and inexperience and prayed for discretion to lead God's people. How do you think about the gifts, skills, and talents God has given you? How can you focus on using them for the benefit of the people God has placed in your life?

## Solomon Given Wealth (1:14–17)

The Chronicler displays the glory of Solomon's peaceful reign. This foreshadows the eternal reign of the Messiah, David's Son, and would encourage the returned exiles to joyously await and pray for His coming.

## Preparing to Build the Temple (2:1–18)

As Solomon prepares to build the temple, he sends a letter to the king of Tyre, requesting timber as well as a skilled craftsman who can execute any design and work with any kind of material.

## Solomon Builds the Temple (3:1–17)

Solomon builds the temple on Mount Moriah at the site David prepared. The inside of the temple is overlaid in gold. The Most Holy Place, God's dwelling place in Israel, is a perfect cube. Here he places two wooden cherubim overlaid with gold, which stand on either side and above the ark.

Mount Moriah was the perfect place for the temple to be built. Abraham's sacrifice of the ram in place of his son and the sacrifices of all the animals at the temple powerfully foreshadow Jesus' death in our place. What things in Holy Communion remind you of the sacrifice Jesus made in our place?

**SET THE SCENE**

**What was significant about Mount Moriah?**

Mount Moriah was the place where Abraham went to offer Isaac as a burnt offering in Genesis 22. At that time, God provided a ram as a substitute for Isaac. This ties together Abraham's sacrifice of Isaac, God's appearance to David in the plague, and Jesus' sacrifice on the cross nearby.

## The Temple's Furnishings (4:1–5:1)

Solomon made an altar of bronze for the burnt offerings, a sea of cast metal for the priests to wash themselves in, ten basins to wash utensils for the sacrifices, ten golden lampstands to light the temple interior, and two pillars for the temple entrance.

## The Ark Brought to the Temple (5:2–14)

What was the significance of the glory of God filling the temple?

How did Jesus fulfill and exceed the temple as the "place" to approach God and receive His mercy?

How does your being a living temple of Christ affect the different aspects of your daily life?

**WAYPOINT**

***What does this text show us?***

During the Feast of Booths, Solomon assembles all Israel to dedicate the temple. The priests carry the ark of the covenant into its place in the temple. When the Levite musicians sing, God's glory fills the temple, as it had filled the tabernacle when Moses first set it up on Mount Sinai.

***What does this text reveal about God's plan of salvation?***

When the ark of the covenant is placed in the Most Holy Place, God fills the temple with the cloud of His presence. When the Son of God became human, He came to dwell among us and gave us access to God through His life, death, and resurrection.

***What does this text uncover about our identity and calling as God's people today?***

Through Baptism, the Holy Trinity dwells within us, making each of us His temple. As we share the Word of God with the people in our lives, Christ is ministering to them; convicting them of their sins; and revealing God's love, mercy, and full forgiveness.

## Solomon Blesses the People (6:1–11)

Solomon reminds the Israelites of God's promise through Moses to place His name upon a city and to dwell there. God has kept His promise and has provided David a son to raise a temple for Him. Now God has placed His name upon Jerusalem and dwells there in Solomon's temple.

## Solomon's Prayer of Dedication (6:12–42)

**VISUALIZE**

Humbly kneeling on a bronze platform, Solomon dedicates the temple as a house of prayer. He asks God to listen to the prayers addressed to Him in this temple. Solomon acknowledges that this small building cannot contain God but asks God to honor it as the one location in Israel to which God's people can look, no matter where they are or what circumstances they are under. Here they can call upon God with confidence that He will hear and answer them.

**LINK BETWEEN THE TESTAMENTS**

**House of Prayer (2 Chronicles 6:20 → Matthew 21:13)**

After each morning and afternoon burnt offering, a priest went inside the temple to burn incense while the people prayed outside. When Jesus cleansed the temple He said that the temple was God's house of prayer for all nations. This burning activity foreshadowed Jesus, through whom our prayers rise like incense to God.

**CLEAR THE CONFUSION**

**Praying from captivity?**

Solomon asked God to hear His people if they were taken captive to a foreign land and prayed toward this temple. From exile, Daniel faced toward Jerusalem and prayed (Daniel 6:10). When he was thrown into the lions' den for praying to the God of Israel, God heard his prayer and shut the lions' mouths.

You may notice in 6:5 that Solomon calls David a "prince." He is reminding himself and all of Israel that God is and always has been their true King and always will be. Why is it important for us to remember that, no matter who rules in our land, Jesus Christ is truly King of kings and Lord of lords?

## Fire from Heaven (7:1–3)

After Solomon's prayer, when the people sing, "For He is good, for His steadfast love endures forever" (v. 3). God sends fire down from heaven (most likely lightning) which consumes the sacrifices. The glory of the Lord enters the temple and the priests are unable to do their work in it.

## The Dedication of the Temple (7:4–10)

Solomon offers a huge number of animals to God. On the eighth day, he holds a sacred assembly. Just as Aaron's ordination lasted a week and his priestly service began on the eighth day, the temple's dedication lasts seven days and then God begins serving His people on the eighth day.

## If My People Pray (7:11–22)

In the night, God promises Solomon He will answer prayers offered toward the temple from repentant hearts. He promises that if Solomon is faithful, like David, a son will always sit on his throne. But if he is unfaithful, God will remove him and cast the temple out of His sight.

God graciously promised Solomon He would hear the faith-filled prayers of His people, especially when they cried out in repentance. What comfort and assurance do you take from God's promise to hear our prayers offered in faith for Jesus' sake?

**PICTURE OF THE SAVIOR**

**The House Cast Out of God's Sight**

Solomon's temple was looted and destroyed because of Judah's disloyalty, then later rebuilt by the returned exiles. Isaiah uses similar language about the Messiah (Isaiah 52:14). Jesus' possessions were divided among the soldiers and lots cast for His tunic. Then, in His resurrection, Jesus was raised in glory.

The arrival of the queen of Sheba with her caravan, guards, and treasures must have amazed the people of Jerusalem, just as the arrival of the Wise Men must have after Jesus was born. She foreshadowed the Gentiles who believed Jesus was the promised Savior and were saved. Think of someone you once thought was unlikely to ever be a believer. What do you find most remarkable about his or her life of faith?

## Solomon's Accomplishments (8:1–18)

Solomon builds store cities and strengthens the cities on his borders. He faithfully celebrates all the festivals and offerings Moses required in Leviticus. Finally, Solomon joins Hiram, king of Tyre, on a shipping trade, which brings vast wealth into his kingdom each year.

## The Queen of Sheba (9:1–12)

The queen of Sheba has heard the stories of Solomon's wealth and wisdom. She comes personally to see for herself and finds that the reality is even greater than what she has been told. The queen declares that God loves Israel and that is why He set Solomon as king over them.

### LINK BETWEEN THE TESTAMENTS

**The Queen of Sheba (2 Chronicles 9:1–12 → Matthew 12:42)**

Jesus mentioned this queen of Sheba, a Gentile who traveled great distances to hear Solomon's wisdom. She would have traveled even farther to hear Jesus the Messiah, but the Jewish leaders heard Jesus and refused to repent or believe. On the Last Day, she will condemn those who refused to listen to Him.

## Solomon's Wealth (9:13–28)

Solomon's reign marks a golden age in Israel because of the peace, wealth, and worship established in Jerusalem. This high point foreshadows the eternal reign of Jesus Christ, when He returns to judge the living and the dead, restore God's creation, and establish His eternal reign on earth.

Picturing the wealth and splendor of Solomon's temple and palace is one way for us to picture the glories of Christ's kingdom when He returns. How do you picture the splendor of heaven?

## Solomon's Death (9:29–31)

Chronicles says the rest of Solomon's reign is recorded in writings of the prophets Nathan, Ahijah, and Iddo. These no doubt include Solomon forsaking the Lord to worship the false gods of his many wives. After ruling forty years, Solomon dies and is buried in Jerusalem.

### CLEAR THE CONFUSION

**Why doesn't the book of Chronicles record Solomon's fall from the Lord?**

The Chronicler did not want to detract from the importance and centrality of the temple that Solomon built and the temple worship that took place there.

### SET THE SCENE

**Solomon's Wisdom Writings**

Of the five wisdom books in the Bible (Job, Psalms, Proverbs, Ecclesiastes, and the Song of Solomon), Solomon wrote the majority of the last three and contributed a few psalms.

# Division of the Kingdom of Israel (10:1–12:16)

This section narrates the revolt against Rehoboam and the division of the kingdom. It notes how the Lord secured Rehoboam's kingdom because he welcomed the priests and Levites whom Jeroboam in the north had driven out.

## The Revolt Against Rehoboam (10:1–19)

Rehoboam succeeds Solomon. Jeroboam, son of Nebat, representing the people of Israel, asks him to lighten the burden Solomon had imposed. Rehoboam answers harshly as his young advisers suggest. The people of Israel rebel, and the kingdom is divided against the house of David.

## Rehoboam Secures His Kingdom (11:1–12)

Rehoboam prepares to go to war to retake the tribes of Israel that broke off from him. But when God tells Rehoboam He has brought about this development and commands him not to attack Israel, he obeys. Instead, he fortifies several cities to defend against Jeroboam.

## Priests and Levites Come to Jerusalem (11:13–17)

The exiles would be encouraged by reading about the faithful priests and Levites who had left their towns in the north to resettle in Jerusalem and serve at Solomon's temple. Consider your pastor and other called workers. Where did they come from to serve you? How can you encourage and support them in their labors?

In the north, Jeroboam builds two temples to keep his subjects from going to the Jerusalem temple and returning their loyalty to David's king. He has also expelled the rightful priests and the Levites. These go to Jerusalem to serve the true God, strengthening Rehoboam's reign.

## Rehoboam's Family (11:18–23)

Though Chronicles does not mention the many wives of Solomon, it does mention Rehoboam's many wives. Rehoboam chooses Abijah to succeed him as king.

## Egypt Plunders Jerusalem (12:1–16)

For three years, Rehoboam is faithful to God (11:17). Then he and Judah forsake God. In the fifth year of his reign, God brings up the Egyptians. Rehoboam and the people repent, and God is merciful to them. The Egyptians take the wealth from Solomon's bounty, but let the people remain.

# The Davidic Dynasty Before the Assyrian Invasion (13:1–26:23)

This section traces the line of David between the death of Rehoboam and the Assyrian invasion. We learn of good kings who are devoted to the Lord and of the influence of the kings of the north when Jehoshaphat, king of Judah, makes an alliance with Israel's wicked King Ahab.

## Abijah Reigns in Judah (13:1–22)

Despite facing an overwhelming army from Jeroboam, Abijah warns the ten tribes they have forsaken God, His temple, and His appointed priests to worship idols. When Jeroboam attacks, Judah cries out to God for help, and God delivers them.

## Asa Reigns in Judah (14:1–15)

**VISUALIZE**

Abijah's son Asa enjoyed ten years of peace because he removed all idols and wholeheartedly served the Lord. When Judah was invaded by an overwhelming force from Ethiopia, Asa cried out to the Lord, and God drove out the invaders.

## Asa's Religious Reforms (15:1–19)

After the prophet Azariah proclaims that God has given Judah victory and peace because they drew near to Him, Asa is encouraged. Together with his people and those Israelites who left the Northern Kingdom to seek the Lord in Judah, Asa promises to dedicate themselves to serve God.

The high places were a slippery slope for Israel. They started as places to worship the God of Israel, but without proper oversight from the priests and Levites, these high places degenerated into false worship and then worship of false gods. Where are the "high places" at which Christians worship today?

CLEAR THE CONFUSION

**What were the high places?**

High places were hilltops or mountaintops where sacrifices were made. Before the temple was built, the Israelites used these places to worship God. This practice was so entrenched that the people clung to the custom even after Solomon built the temple. We will see many upright kings of Judah unsuccessfully try to break the people of this habit.

## Asa's Last Years (16:1–14)

When Baasha, king of the northern ten tribes, comes to blockade Judah, Asa seeks help from the king of Syria instead of God. When the prophet Hanani confronts him, Asa imprisons and mistreats him.

## Jehoshaphat Reigns in Judah (17:1–19)

Jehoshaphat, Asa's son, wholeheartedly devotes himself to God, as King David had done before him. He also sends officials, priests, and Levites to teach God's Law to the people of Judah. God blesses him by making him more and more prosperous and giving him peace.

## Jehoshaphat Allies with Ahab (18:1–27)

Jehoshaphat foolishly allies himself with Israel's most wicked king, Ahab, promising to join in a fight against one of Ahab's enemies. Jehoshaphat insists on consulting a prophet of the Lord before the battle. Ahab is not pleased with the prophet's counsel.

On Mount Sinai, God had forbidden the Israelites to marry unbelievers (Exodus 34:12–16). He wanted to protect believers from relationships that would lure them away from Him. Looking back over your life, how have your friendships and relationships with unbelievers affected your walk with Jesus Christ?

CLEAR THE CONFUSION

**What were marriage alliances?**

Jehoshaphat married his son Jehoram to Ahab's wicked daughter Athaliah to bring an end to the generations-long wars with the Northern Kingdom. This may have stopped the Northern Kingdom from invading Judah, but Athaliah nearly destroyed the entire line of David leading to Jesus Christ.

## The Defeat and Death of Ahab (18:28–34)

### VISUALIZE

Ahab convinced Jehoshaphat to go into battle dressed in his royal robes while he went into battle disguised as a common soldier. God protected Jehoshaphat when he cried out to Him, but Ahab couldn't hide from the eyes of God, who fulfilled His word through Micaiah by a "random" arrow.

### SET THE SCENE

**Why was Ahab propped up in his chariot?**

Ahab's commanders knew that if Israel's warriors saw their king slumped over or absent from his chariot, they would lose courage and be likely to flee in panic. But with Ahab propped up in his chariot, the soldiers looking at his chariot from a distance would think he was still alive and leading the battle.

## Jehoshaphat's Reforms (19:1–11)

God sends a prophet to rebuke Jehoshaphat for allying himself with a king who hated the Lord. As a result, Jehoshaphat institutes many reforms in Judah, charging the judges and officials to fear God and give fair judgments. He also upholds the high priest as Israel's spiritual leader.

## Jehoshaphat's Prayer (20:1–23)

When Jehoshaphat and Judah learn that armies from Moab, Ammon, and Edom are invading from the southeast, they gather at the temple in Jerusalem to call on God to save them. The Spirit speaks through a prophet to assure them of God's protection.

## The LORD Delivers Judah (20:24–34)

God gives the Moabites, Ammonites, and Edomites into Judah's hands. Jehoshaphat gathers the people of Judah at the temple to praise God.

God caused Judah's neighbors to fear them, so Jehoshaphat and his people enjoyed a prolonged peace. We are often not aware of the peace and protection God gives us. Consider some close calls when you could have been badly hurt but God protected you.

God causes all the surrounding nations to fear Judah, so the king and people live in peace throughout the rest of Jehoshaphat's reign.

## The End of Jehoshaphat's Reign (20:35–37)

One more time, Jehoshaphat foolishly allies himself with Ahaziah, Ahab's son. As a result, the shipping fleet they construct together is destroyed. Jehoshaphat dies and his son Jehoram reigns in his place.

## Jehoram Reigns in Judah (21:1–20)

Chronicles shows the devastating influence Athaliah has on Jehoram. Jehoram murders his brothers to secure his throne and leads Judah into idolatry. The Northern Kingdom's famous prophet Elijah sends a letter calling on him to repent, but Jehoram does not listen.

The fallout of Jehoshaphat's alliance with Ahab continues in the third generation, as his grandson Ahaziah goes to visit his uncle Joram, the wounded king of Israel, right at the time Jehu is destroying the house of Ahab by God's command. How can we find courage in Christ when we suffer the consequences and fallout from bad decisions in our lives?

## Ahaziah Reigns in Judah (22:1–9)

Counseled by his wicked mother, Athaliah, Ahaziah continues in his father's footsteps, doing evil in God's eyes. God orchestrates his downfall through Jehu as he wipes out the house of Ahab (2 Kings 8:25–9:28).

## Athaliah Reigns in Judah (22:10–12)

Evil Athaliah seizes Judah's throne and, like her husband, murders all the rivals to the throne. Satan tries once again to exterminate the line of David to break God's promise to send the Christ. But one son, Joash, is saved by his aunt and hidden in the temple courts for six years.

### PICTURE OF THE SAVIOR

**Rejected, Persecuted, and Hunted**

Three times Satan used Jehoshaphat's marriage alliance in an attempt to destroy David's line leading to Jesus Christ. Jehoshaphat's son Jehoram murdered all his brothers; his grandson Ahaziah alone survived when Arabians invaded; and Athaliah killed all his great-grandsons except Joash.

During Jesus' earthly life, Satan made many attempts to kill Jesus: King Herod murdered the boys of Bethlehem (Matthew 2:16); in Nazareth, His boyhood neighbors tried to throw Him off a cliff (Luke 4:28–30); twice the people of Jerusalem tried to stone Him (John 8:59; 10:31). But when the Jewish leaders finally killed Jesus on the cross, His suffering and death brought the world salvation. His resurrection on the third day completely conquered Satan.

## Joash Made King (23:1–11)

When Joash is old enough, the priest Jehoiada assembles military commanders and Levite temple guards at the temple in Jerusalem and restores the throne to Joash, the rightful heir of David.

Jehoiada the priest showed great faith in God by hiding Joash for six years and then choosing the moment to gather the commanders, Levites, and leaders to proclaim Joash king. What is the most courageous thing God has empowered you to do?

**CLEAR THE CONFUSION**

**How did Jehoiada the priest benefit from David's organization of the kingdom, as recorded in 1 Chronicles?**

Jehoiada the priest used David's careful organization in 1 Chronicles 23–27 to gather several divisions of soldiers, priests, and Levites together at the same time in Jerusalem. With this military force, he ended Athaliah's usurping reign and put David's rightful heir back on the throne.

## Athaliah Executed (23:12–15)

Hearing the shouting, music, and celebration, Athaliah goes into the house of the Lord to investigate. Seeing the boy king, she has the gall to cry out "Treason! Treason!"—when, in fact, she is the treasonous one.

## Jehoiada's Reforms (23:16–21)

Since Joash is only seven years old at the beginning of his reign, Jehoiada the priest acts as his regent and enacts important reforms to turn Judah back to the Lord its God, especially after two generations of corruption and neglect from the wicked house of Ahab.

## Joash Repairs the Temple (24:1–19)

When Joash is old enough to reign, he restores the temple, which has been neglected since the time of Jehoshaphat. Joash is faithful to the Lord until Jehoiada dies. Then, he listens to the younger princes and abandons the Lord and His temple and serves the Asherim.

Several times in 2 Chronicles the temple is neglected and must be cleansed and repaired. How well are your church facilities maintained? Why is it important not to neglect them?

**CLEAR THE CONFUSION**

**What were the Asherim?**

Representations of Asherah, the most important Canaanite goddess. Asherah was the sister-wife of Baal. She was considered a goddess of fertility and provider of fertile fields and material prosperity. Moses commanded Israel to destroy all Baal idols and Asherah poles in Canaan.

## Joash's Treachery (24:20–22)

The Holy Spirit stirred Zechariah, Jehoiada's son, to warn Joash that God was forsaking him. Despite all Jehoiada had done for him, Joash commanded the people to stone Zechariah to death.

Joash learned what it was to fall into the hands of the living God as he watched a small army overwhelm his much larger army and found himself severely wounded. Yet this was a last wake-up call from God for the king, a last call to repentance. What troubles in your life has God used to turn you from sin and bring you closer to Jesus?

## Joash Assassinated (24:23–27)

Earlier, God defended Judah from overwhelming armies that invaded. Now, the same year Joash had Zechariah stoned to death, God hands Judah over to a small army from Syria. They destroy all the princes who led Joash astray and wound Joash, who is assassinated by servants.

## Amaziah Reigns in Judah (25:1–4)

Amaziah kills the servants who assassinated his father, but, obeying the Law of Moses, he does not kill their children.

## Amaziah's Victories (25:5–13)

Preparing to go to war against Edom, Amaziah finds he only has 300,000 soldiers, so he hires 100,000 men from Ephraim. After being warned by God, he sends them away. Because Amaziah trusts God, God gives him victory over the people of Edom.

## Amaziah's Idolatry (25:14–16)

Unlike any king of Judah before him, Amaziah takes the idols of Edom, the nation God just defeated through him, and sets them up as his own gods. When an unnamed prophet rebukes him, Amaziah orders him to be silent. The prophet announces that God will destroy him.

### Israel Defeats Amaziah (25:17–28)

In arrogant pride, Amaziah challenges Israel to a battle. Joash, king of Israel, warns him, but Amaziah persists and is beaten in battle. He is captured, a large stretch of the wall of Jerusalem is torn down, and the temple is looted.

Chronicles carries many lessons for the returned exiles and for us as well. Under Nehemiah's oversight, the walls of Jerusalem, which the Babylonians had torn down, were rebuilt. But if they abandoned God, He would be against them as well. What warning does God give us in this passage?

### Uzziah Reigns in Judah (26:1–15)

Uzziah begins his reign trusting and serving the Lord. He sets himself to seek the Lord and prospers as a result. He becomes powerful and victorious against the Philistines.

### Uzziah's Pride and Punishment (26:16–23)

Uzziah becomes proud because of his victories. Though not a priest, he enters the temple with a censor to burn incense. Courageous priests stand against him since God chose Aaron's descendants to be priests. When Uzziah becomes angry at their resistance, God strikes him with leprosy.

**The Prophet Isaiah Comes on the Scene**

Isaiah is called as God's prophet during the reign of Uzziah. His ministry continues through the reigns of Uzziah's son Jotham, grandson Ahaz, and great-grandson Hezekiah (Isaiah 1:1).

## Invasions and the Fall of the Davidic Dynasty (27:1–36:23)

In this section, Judah is ruled by mostly evil kings, though two of its most faithful arise late in the era. Finally, God punishes Judah's evil by leading them into exile. The Chronicles end with Cyrus of Persia freeing the exiles and urging them to rebuild the Lord's temple in Jerusalem.

Jotham was a good king who worshiped God but seemed to do nothing to address the corrupt practices the people of Judah had learned from the years Athaliah had been in the throne room of Judah. Why is it important for each of us to look beyond our own personal faith walk and encourage one another to turn from our sins and follow Christ?

### Jotham Reigns in Judah (27:1–9)

Jotham is a good king and serves God like his father, Uzziah, without falling into Uzziah's pride. Like all good kings throughout Chronicles, he builds up the city. But the Chronicler points out that the people still follow corrupt practices.

## Ahaz Reigns in Judah (28:1–4)

Ahaz, Jotham's son, is one of the most wicked kings of Judah. He makes metal images of Baal and even sacrifices his sons as offerings to Baal, burning them to death.

## Judah Defeated (28:5–21)

To bring Ahaz to repentance, God hands Judah over to the kings of Syria and Israel. Many citizens are taken prisoner by Israel until God sends a prophet to intervene. Ahaz also sees his southeastern border invaded by the Edomites and his southwestern border by the Philistines.

### SET THE SCENE

**"Ask a sign of the LORD your God" (Isaiah 7:11).**

Right when Ahaz suffered these crushing defeats and was fearful of the armies of Israel and Syria, God sent Isaiah to promise that He would deliver Judah from their enemies. God even offered to perform a miracle, but Ahaz refused.

So God gave Ahaz a sign: "Behold, the virgin shall conceive and bear a son, and shall call His name Immanuel" (Isaiah 7:14).

## Ahaz's Idolatry (28:22–27)

Following his defeat by the Syrians, Ahaz sacrifices to the gods of Syria's capital city, Damascus. Then, he destroys the vessels of the temple and shuts up its doors. Instead of worshiping the God of Israel, he sets up altars in every corner of Jerusalem to serve false gods.

## Hezekiah Reigns in Judah (29:1–2)

When Ahaz dies, his son Hezekiah becomes king, and he is an exceptional king. For the first time, we see the Chronicler say of a descendant of David: "He did what was right in the eyes of the LORD, according to all that David his father had done" (v. 2).

## Hezekiah Cleanses the Temple (29:3–19)

**VISUALIZE**

Hezekiah's very first acts as king were to reopen the temple doors, direct the Levites to cleanse the temple of the foreign gods, and restore the daily temple service as God had commanded through Moses. It took sixteen days to cleanse the temple and restore its rightful service.

Hezekiah's first priority was to restore daily temple worship. Undoubtedly, he had spent years under his father, awaiting the day he would have the authority to make things right. What are some things you would like to see made right but as of today, you can only watch and pray about?

**PICTURE OF THE SAVIOR**

**Jesus Cleanses the Temple**

Hezekiah likely had to bide his time until God placed him upon the throne. Then when he became king, the first thing he did was cleanse the temple. Jesus must have seen the money changers in the temple year after year, but waited for His Father's timing to cleanse and restore it to its proper service.

## Hezekiah Restores Temple Worship (29:20–36)

Following in David's footsteps, Hezekiah organizes the priests and Levites to restore the proper worship at the temple. The people of Judah are so gladdened by worship that they bring more burnt offerings of their own than there are priests cleansed and ready to offer them.

## Passover Celebrated (30:1–27)

Hezekiah calls on Judah and sends messengers to invite the remnant from the Northern Kingdom of Israel who have escaped exile in Assyria to come to Jerusalem to celebrate the Passover. This is the biggest Passover celebration in Jerusalem since the days of Solomon.

God commanded a tithe from the Israelites to provide for the Levites and their families so the Levites could do their duties full-time. The Levites, in turn, gave a tithe of this tithe to the priests, providing for their needs so the priests could dedicate themselves to serve the Lord and His people full-time. How do we benefit when we properly support our pastors and church workers as God requires of us?

The defeat and withdrawal of Sennacherib's army led to Hezekiah receiving honor and praise from other nations that no longer felt threatened by Assyria. How does Jesus' death and resurrection cause us to offer Him similar honor and praise? What no longer threatens us?

## Hezekiah Organizes the Priests (31:1–21)

The people of Judah remove the idols throughout Judah and the former Northern Kingdom. The people bring their tithes so the Levites and priests can serve full-time. Hezekiah's spiritual renewal will prove crucial when Assyrian officials try to intimidate the people of Jerusalem.

## Sennacherib Invades Judah (32:1–8)

King Sennacherib invades Judah with his undefeated Assyrian armies. Hezekiah stops the springs of water outside Jerusalem, rebuilds the walls, and fortifies the cities. Instead of assuring people to trust these preparations, Hezekiah tells them to trust their God.

## Sennacherib Blasphemes (32:9–19)

While attacking the important city of Lachish in Judah, Sennacherib sends his servants to intimidate and threaten Hezekiah and the people of Jerusalem, hoping they will surrender. The servants blaspheme the Lord, comparing Him to the false gods of the nations they defeated.

## The LORD Delivers Jerusalem (32:20–23)

The prophet Isaiah and Hezekiah pray, and God sends His angel who single-handedly destroys the power of the Assyrian army. Sennacherib returns to his own land in shame. Hezekiah is honored by the nations around Judah, just as David and Solomon had been.

## Hezekiah's Pride and Achievements (32:24–33)

Hezekiah becomes ill to the point of death, and God hears his prayer and heals him. Rather than humbly praising God for delivering him from death, the king becomes puffed up with pride, and God disciplines him. Hezekiah repents and goes on to prosper by God's mercy.

## Manasseh Reigns in Judah (33:1–9)

With the death of Hezekiah, we move from one of the most faithful kings of Judah to the single most unfaithful: Manasseh, Hezekiah's son. The Chronicler gives a sad list of the evils Manasseh reintroduces to Judah, including setting up idols in the temple and sacrificing his own children.

## Manasseh's Repentance (33:10–20)

God brings up the Assyrians, who capture Manasseh and take him prisoner. In the distress of his captivity, he finally repents. In great mercy, God restores him to his kingdom, and Manasseh removes the idols and their altars and restores proper worship.

How can God's forgiveness and restoration of Manasseh reassure you when you suffer from the consequences of your sins?

### CLEAR THE CONFUSION

**Why did God restore Manasseh?**

God restored Manasseh because of His great love and mercy. He delights not in condemning and destroying sinners but in saving them for the sake of His Son, Jesus Christ. Manasseh's repentance and restoration gives us comfort and reassurance that God forgives our worst sins for Jesus' sake.

## Amon's Reign and Death (33:21–25)

During Manasseh's long reign, the people of Judah had followed his lead, completely abandoning their devotion to the Lord. Manasseh's son Amon continues in Manasseh's rebellion against God, having learned nothing from his father's imprisonment and repentance.

## Josiah Reigns in Judah (34:1–7)

When Amon is assassinated, the last faithful king of Judah, eight-year-old Josiah, begins his reign. When sixteen, he begins to seek the Lord as David had done. When twenty, Josiah destroys the carved images, the idols, and the altars to false gods throughout Judah and Israel.

When Hezekiah learned the Babylonians would conquer Jerusalem and take his descendants prisoner, Hezekiah only thought about himself, happy that he would die before that day would come (2 Kings 20:16–19). Josiah, on the other hand, worked hard to renew the covenant, remove the idols, and restore the people's relationship with the Lord. How can we reflect Josiah's concern for his fellow believers and the coming generations?

## The Book of the Law Found (34:8–21)

When Josiah orders the temple to be ceremonially cleansed and restored, the priests find the Book of the Law. When they read it to King Josiah, he responds in grief, fear, and humility and consults a prophet to learn if there is any way to turn God from His wrath.

## Huldah Prophesies Disaster (34:22–33)

The prophetess Huldah informs Josiah that Manasseh's sins cannot be forgiven until God pours out His wrath on Judah for their unfaithfulness. But since Josiah is grieved, God promises that destruction will not happen during Josiah's day. Josiah rededicates himself to serve God.

## Josiah Keeps the Passover (35:1–19)

Josiah observes the Passover exactly as Moses had commanded. Such a Passover has not been celebrated since the time of Samuel. This shows us how closely and carefully Josiah read the books of Exodus and Leviticus.

### CLEAR THE CONFUSION

**Why were the Levites carrying around the ark of the covenant (35:3)?**

During the reigns of Manasseh and Amon, the ark must have been removed from the place Solomon had prepared for it in the Most Holy Place. Perhaps it was put in storage and brought out for special festivals. Josiah commanded the priests to return the ark to its proper place permanently.

God warned Josiah not to interfere with the king of Egypt. When have you found it hard to know how God was guiding you in a specific situation? What are some ways you can ask God to guide you?

## Josiah Killed in Battle (35:20–27)

Sadly, Josiah's reign is cut short when he goes to battle against the king of Egypt. Even though God warns him through Pharaoh not to interfere with Egypt's attack on Babylon, which is a rising world power, Josiah disguises himself and leads his army against the Egyptians.

## Judah's Decline (36:1–16)

After Josiah's death, Judah quickly spirals to its destruction. The Chronicler briefly recalls the tragic reigns of three of Josiah's sons and one of his grandsons. All of these kings are wicked, rebelling against God and refusing to obey God's warnings from His prophets.

## Jerusalem Captured and Burned (36:17–21)

### VISUALIZE

To punish the rebelliousness and evil of Judah, God brings up the king of the Chaldeans, or Babylon. Many young men are killed, and the survivors are carried off into exile to be servants or slaves in Babylon. The temple is looted and burned to the ground, along with the king's palaces. The temple's and the king's treasures are taken to Babylon. The land rests seventy years until the rise of the Persian Empire.

### SET THE SCENE

**The Prophet Jeremiah and the Fall of Jerusalem**

In our fourth volume, *The Books of the Prophets*, we will discuss the writings of the prophet Jeremiah. Jeremiah was the prophet God raised up in these last days of Judah. He began serving in the years of Josiah and continued as the prophet counseling each of the final four kings to repent, but they would not listen. He prophesied that the land would lie desolate for seventy years before God would allow the exiles to return to rebuild Jerusalem. He even named Cyrus and his decree more than seventy years before the Persian emperor was known or rose to power.

## The Proclamation of Cyrus (36:22–23)

Seventy years after the first group of exiles were dragged away from Jerusalem, the Persian emperor Cyrus issues a decree acknowledging the Lord, the God of heaven, and sharing God's charge to build a house at Jerusalem. He encourages the exiled Jews to return to Jerusalem to rebuild the temple.

# EZRA

## Welcome to Ezra

In Ezra, we learn how God fulfills His promise to bring His people from exile in Babylon back to the Promised Land. We see the people of Judah struggling to rebuild the temple and reestablish themselves and their community amid the turmoils of politics on an empire-wide scale. We follow along as leaders like Ezra seek to live out their faith while surrounded by so much opposition. Most importantly, we witness God's faithfulness to His people over more than eighty years, as they return from exile and await the coming of the Messiah, who would be born in their midst some five hundred years later.

What do you know about the book of Ezra? What do you hope to learn by reading through and considering this book?

## Ezra at a Glance

- **Start:** The book of Ezra begins with Cyrus's decree to send the exiled Judeans back to the Promised Land to rebuild the temple in 538 BC.
- **End:** The book of Ezra concludes with the scribe Ezra's reforms around 458 BC.
- **Theme:** God uses the political forces of the day to bring about the return from exile so that the temple could be rebuilt in anticipation of the Messiah, who would be born in that land to that people.
- **Author and Date:** Ezra likely wrote the book, using various sources, around 440 BC.
- **Places Visited:** Persia, Jerusalem, the province Beyond the River, Babylon
- **Journey Time:** The ten chapters of Ezra can be read in about an hour.
- **Outline:**
  - First Return of Exiles and Rebuilding of the Temple (1:1–6:22)
  - Second Return of Exiles Under Ezra (7:1–8:36)
  - Ezra's Reforms Ban Intermarriage (9:1–10:44)

## Five Top Sights and Spectacles of Ezra

**The King's Decree (1:1–11)** Marvel at how God uses Cyrus, the pagan Persian king, to release the Judeans from exile and send them back to the Promised Land.

**Rebuilding the Temple (3:8–13)** Watch as the foundations of the temple in Jerusalem are laid and the people respond to God's grace.

**Israel's Courage (5:1–5)** Discover how God's prophets spur on the work of building the temple, despite the threats from hostile neighbors.

**The Temple Is Dedicated (6:13–22)** Observe God's people, after more than a decade of struggle and delays, finally dedicate the temple and celebrate the Passover together.

**Ezra's Caravan (7:1–28)** Witness Ezra—a scribe, priest, and secretary to the king—rally a second wave of exiles to return to Jerusalem.

## Seeing Jesus in Ezra

The book of Ezra begins with a decree from the king of Persia that the exiles can return home. God uses the unbelieving powers of the world to enact His grand plan of salvation. The people of God will return to their land, rebuild the temple, and await the coming of the Messiah, Jesus Christ. God will bring salvation to the world through the nation of His people, and it will happen in the land He had promised to Abraham. The point of the return from exile, then, is ultimately all about Jesus.

## First Return of Exiles and Rebuilding of the Temple (1:1–6:22)

The first section of Ezra outlines the first wave of exiles returning from Persia under the leadership of Zerubbabel and Jeshua, beginning around 538 BC. Many times under different Persian kings adversaries try to halt the rebuilding progress. Finally the temple is completed.

### The Proclamation of Cyrus (1:1–11)

What stands out to you about Cyrus's edict? Why?

God leads the Persian king Cyrus to free the Judeans to return to Jerusalem and rebuild the house of God. The Lord stirs up the hearts of a small, faithful group to return. Cyrus gives them the temple furnishings that had been carried away from the temple by the Babylonians.

### CLEAR THE CONFUSION

**What happened to Babylon? Why are the Persians in charge?**

The Babylonian Empire was conquered by a coalition of Medes and Persians about seventy years after Jerusalem was destroyed and the people of Judah were taken into exile. The Medes and Persians conquered Babylon, and Cyrus of Persia was the first ruler of this new Persian Empire.

## The Exiles Return (2:1–70)

### VISUALIZE

More than 40,000 Judeans answered the call to return to Jerusalem. Of these, more than 4,200 were priests. Only 341 Levites, who served the priests and fulfilled other religious duties, returned. This would cause issues moving forward.

Why do you suppose that so few Levites returned in this first wave?

### SET THE SCENE

**How many exiled Judeans returned to Jerusalem?**

Ezra's account lists more than 40,000 people, but the vast majority of exiles refused to face the hardships of returning to Canaan and rebuilding the temple. By the time of Christ's birth, the population of Jews living in Alexandria, Egypt, was greater than those in Jerusalem.

## Rebuilding the Altar (3:1–7)

Within a year of returning, the Israelites rebuilt the altar of the Lord in Jerusalem and began reinstating the worship and ceremonial practices Moses had recorded in Leviticus. Their leaders were Zerubbabel, grandson of King Jehoiachin (see 2 Chronicles 36:9–10), who would later be governor of Judea, and the high priest Jeshua.

## Rebuilding the Temple (3:8–13)

The following year, the Judeans work to reestablish Levitical practices and lay the foundations of the new temple in Jerusalem. Some people shout and praise the Lord, but some weep with sadness.

Have you been present when a foundation was laid for a house, church, or other building? What emotions are experienced?

### CLEAR THE CONFUSION

**Why were people weeping when the foundation was laid?**

Some may have recalled the sin that had led to the first temple being destroyed. Others knew the appearance of this temple would never match the majestic grandeur of Solomon's temple. Regardless, the laying of the foundation was bittersweet for many, and joy was mixed with sadness.

### PICTURE OF THE SAVIOR

**Rebuilding the Temple**

The temple represented God dwelling in the midst of His people. It prefigured Jesus Christ, the Son of God, who became human and came to dwell among us in His human body. Just as the temple was destroyed by the Babylonians and raised again by the returned exiles, Jesus would be put to death on the cross and rise to life again on the third day.

## Adversaries Oppose the Rebuilding (4:1–6)

When the people of the land offer to help in the construction of the temple, the Judeans refuse, knowing that God has commanded them to rebuild it. Spurned, the people of the land use both legal means and threats to thwart the construction of the temple over the next fifteen years.

Why do you suppose the author of Ezra included accounts of this fierce opposition of the local inhabitants to the rebuilding of the temple? How does it help prepare us for the opposition we will face as followers of Christ?

**SET THE SCENE**

**The People of the Land**

When the Assyrians destroyed the Northern Kingdom of Israel, they exiled the Israelites and resettled conquered peoples of different regions and nations in northern Israel. It would have been unthinkable for these people to be permitted to have any part in the construction of the new temple.

**CLEAR THE CONFUSION**

**Two letters in the wrong order?**

In chapters 4–6, Ezra gives us the text of two official letters sent to two different Persian kings. The letter in chapter 4 was written at least two decades after the letter in chapter 5. Ezra's main point in these chapters was not the order in which building projects were attempted (temple first, then city wall and other buildings) but the fierce opposition the returned exiles faced as they sought to rebuild the temple and Jerusalem as God willed.

The following chart presents a basic timeline to help clarify the order of events that take place in Ezra:

| CHAPTERS | PERSIAN EMPEROR | MAIN ACTIVITY |
|---|---|---|
| 1–3 | Cyrus | Temple construction begun |
| | Cambyses | Temple construction halted |
| 5–6 | Darius I | Temple completed |
| | Ahasuerus (Xerxes) | Events in Esther |
| 4 | Artaxerxes | City walls and building foundations |

## The Letter to King Artaxerxes (4:7–16)

This letter is written decades after the temple is completed to Artaxerxes, the son of Ahasuerus (Esther's king), who is ruling Persia. Leaders from the region that included Judea are trying to stop the rebuilding of Jerusalem's walls and the construction of other buildings in the city.

**CLEAR THE CONFUSION**

**What rebellions did the historical records show?**

If Artaxerxes had access to Babylonian records, he could easily find the accounts of three times that Judah's kings and people violated oaths they had made with Babylonian kings (2 Kings 24:1, 20; 25:25–26). Judah clearly had a history of rebellion, which had to be taken seriously.

## The King Orders the Work to Cease (4:17–24)

**VISUALIZE**

Artaxerxes wrote a letter back to this coalition of Judah's adversaries. After consulting the historical records, which showed Judah had been a rebellious people, he issued a decree to stop all work on rebuilding the walls. The adversaries not only stopped the construction, they tore down the walls and burned the gates. The book of Nehemiah explains how God overcame this opposition and assured the rebuilding of Jerusalem's walls.

What do you know about the prophets Haggai and Zechariah? How might this mention of their work in Ezra help you better understand their writings as minor prophets?

## Rebuilding Begins Anew (5:1–5)

Returning to the temple reconstruction, Ezra explains how the prophets Haggai and Zechariah roused Zerubbabel the governor and Jeshua the high priest to resume rebuilding the temple. The Persian governor Tattenai permits construction to continue while he consults King Darius.

## Tattenai's Letter to King Darius (5:6–17)

Tattenai reports to Darius the rebuilding work being done in Jerusalem and the Judeans' claims for the legality of their endeavor. Tattenai prompts the king to search the records for Cyrus's original decree to legitimize their work.

## The Decree of Darius (6:1–12)

When Cyrus's decree is found, Darius writes back to Tattenai decreeing that the funding for the temple construction and operation will be provided by royal revenue from Tattenai's province. In addition, any opposition will be punished by death.

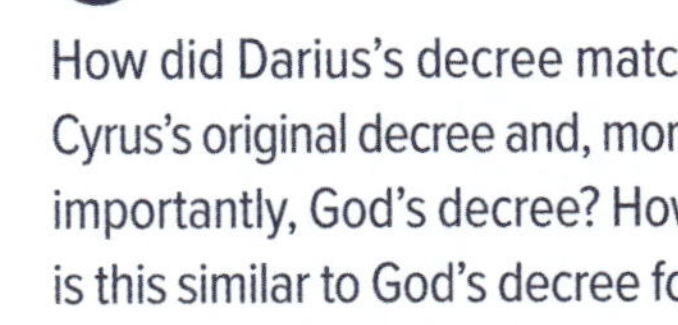

How did Darius's decree match Cyrus's original decree and, more importantly, God's decree? How is this similar to God's decree for all sinners to believe in Jesus Christ, the only Lord and Savior?

## The Temple Finished and Dedicated (6:13–18)

**VISUALIZE**

The decree came to pass, and the temple was finished and dedicated in Jerusalem. There was much rejoicing and celebration.

**PICTURE OF THE SAVIOR**

**The Rebuilt Temple**

All of God's promises attached to the temple of Solomon, and the tabernacle before it, applied to this temple also. That makes the temple a picture of the Savior. When Jesus rose from the dead on the third day, His resurrected body was the same body first given to Him by God in the womb of Mary.

## Passover Celebrated (6:19–22)

After the dedication, Passover is joyously celebrated by the returned exiles. They celebrate the Passover with all its regulations and requirements given by Moses. The Judeans also praise God for turning the heart of the king to help them finish the temple.

# Second Return of Exiles Under Ezra (7:1–8:36)

The second main division of the book focuses on a second wave of exiles who return under the leadership of Ezra the scribe. The focus of the book from here on is Ezra's work to teach the returned exiles the Law of God.

## Ezra Sent to Teach the People (7:1–28)

**WAYPOINT**

***What does this text show us?***
Fifty years after the completion of the temple, the Lord inspires Ezra, a priest, scribe, and royal secretary, to request Persian King Artaxerxes's permission to go to Jerusalem to bolster the people of Jerusalem. The king sends Ezra with royal documents.

***What does this text reveal about God's plan of salvation?***
God sends Ezra, an expert in the Law of God, to teach His truth. The people of Judea needed to be sustained by God's Word. As they heard the promises and messages of God, they would cling in faith to God's promise to send a Savior, who would forgive them their sins.

***What does this text uncover about our identity and calling as God's people today?***
Through the Word of God, the Holy Spirit creates and sustains faith. God's people always need to continually learn His truth from His Word. Just as God provided for the physical needs of the exiles, even more so He provided for their spiritual needs through His Word. He does the same for us today.

What details stick out to you about Ezra's character from this section? Why is that?

What are things that can happen to Christians when they abandon the truth of God's Word for the teachings of the world?

How can we as Christians today build up the habit of meditating on God's Word and make it more a part of our daily lives?

## Genealogy of Those Who Returned with Ezra (8:1–14)

Ezra records the names of the families that join him in relocating to Jerusalem. Some of these names are of the royal family of David, showing how God had preserved the remnant of David's house.

## Ezra Sends for Levites (8:15–20)

Ezra recounts his preparations before leaving for Jerusalem. Concerned about the lack of Levites in the expedition, Ezra locates some who will join him to serve in the temple in Jerusalem.

### Fasting and Prayer for Protection (8:21–23)

Ezra recounts the time of fasting and prayer he proclaimed for their caravan. Since Ezra has told the king that God would protect them and their vast treasure on the journey and thus they did not need guards, Ezra and the people fast and pray for protection before their journey.

### Priests to Guard Offerings (8:24–36)

Ezra gives specific duties to the priests and Levites to keep the treasures safe on their journey. God protects the caravan all the way to Jerusalem. Ezra and the priests pause for three days of prayer and praise. The treasures are given to the temple, and the returned exiles offer many sacrifices.

Consider what it would have been like to be part of that caravan. How would it have impacted your understanding of being part of the community of God's people?

## Ezra's Reforms Ban Intermarriage (9:1–10:44)

The final section of Ezra shows the turmoil and struggle of Judea's teacher in working to bring God's people back to faithful living.

### Ezra Prays About Intermarriage (9:1–15)

Ezra learns that the returned exiles had intermarried with the pagan people of the land. He tears his clothes and hair, and he fasts. He earnestly prays to God to turn from His wrath and forgive the guilt of the people who have not held fast to God's commandment.

### The People Confess Their Sin (10:1–17)

The men are moved to repentance by Ezra's passionate confession and prayer. Ezra gathers the faithful Israelites and proclaims that they should make confession and separate from unbelieving spouses. Ezra and the officials take three months to cleanse the impurity from each city.

How did the leaders of the Jews balance their zeal to act immediately with the prudence to do things in good order? What can we learn from their example as God's people today?

### Those Guilty of Intermarriage (10:18–44)

The book concludes with a record of the 111 illegal marriages that were annulled as a result of the investigation.

# NEHEMIAH

## Welcome to Nehemiah

In the Hebrew Scriptures, the books of Nehemiah and Ezra are paired together and recorded on the same scroll. Ezra, a priest, records the difficulties of rebuilding the temple and then the task of restoring the temple to its place as the spiritual center for the people. Nehemiah, a layman, uses his gifts of leadership and encouragement to restore the protective walls surrounding the city.

What do you know about the book of Nehemiah? What are some specific things you'd like to learn more about?

## Nehemiah at a Glance

- **Start:** Nehemiah receives a report concerning conditions in Jerusalem from a group of exiles who have returned to the Persian capital, Susa.
- **End:** The book concludes when Nehemiah returns to Jerusalem and sets the people back on the path God has intended for them.
- **Theme:** Our sin exiles us from God and from one another. God restores His remnant and brings them together to enjoy His defense and protection. God will bring the promised Savior through this remnant.
- **Author and Date:** Nehemiah, the governor of Judah, wrote the book that bears his name between 445 and 432 BC.
- **Places Visited:** Susa, Jerusalem's gates and walls
- **Journey Time:** The thirteen chapters of Nehemiah can be read in approximately one hour.
- **Outline:**
  - Nehemiah's First Visit and Rebuilding of Jerusalem's Walls (1:1–12:47)
  - Nehemiah's Second Visit: Problems and Solutions (13:1–31)

# Five Top Sights and Spectacles of Nehemiah

**Nehemiah Is Commissioned by Artaxerxes and Inspects Jerusalem (2:1–20)** Follow along as Nehemiah uses his connection to the king to learn more about the needs in Jerusalem.

**Nehemiah Directs the Rebuilding of the Wall (3:1–32)** Join the workers as they organize and begin restoring Jerusalem's walls and gates.

**Defending the Rebuilding Efforts (4:1–23)** Rise to the defense of the builders as they resist the efforts to halt the rebuilding.

**Ezra Shares God's Law (8:1–12)** Listen as Ezra reads the Law and leads the people to repentance.

**Renewing the Covenant (10:1–39)** Learn the specifics of the covenant as the people recommit themselves to God's service.

# Seeing Jesus in Nehemiah

Nehemiah's ministry is similar in some aspects to Jesus' ministry. He knew the people needed to hear the message of God's Law before they could fully appreciate the message of God's promised salvation. Nehemiah was a man of prayer who called out to God for help as he encouraged the people to trust in God's promises, just as Jesus prayed and encouraged.

# Nehemiah's First Visit and Rebuilding of Jerusalem's Walls (1:1–12:47)

### The Destruction of Jerusalem

The city of Jerusalem was overrun by the Babylonians in 587 BC. Jeremiah 52:14 reports, "And all the army of the Chaldeans, who were with the captain of the guard, broke down all the walls around Jerusalem." One hundred forty years later, the report came to Nehemiah regarding the desperate conditions in Jerusalem.

## Report from Jerusalem (1:1–3)

Nehemiah, the cupbearer of King Artaxerxes, receives a distressing report from his brother Hanani. The situation for the returned exiles in Jerusalem is quite grim. They are surrounded by enemies but have no protective wall around the city.

### CLEAR THE CONFUSION

**What is a cupbearer?**

The cupbearer was an important and trusted official within the royal court. The cupbearer's primary responsibility was to protect the king from poisoning. In addition, the cupbearer was typically the keeper for the king's signet, or his seal used to mark official documents. He had a close relationship with his king.

## Nehemiah's Prayer (1:4–11)

Troubled by the conditions in Jerusalem, Nehemiah prays to God in repentance on behalf of his own sins as well as those of his family and the nation of Israel. Nehemiah prays for God to bless his coming discussion with King Artaxerxes.

Consider Nehemiah's prayer. Besides himself, whom else does he pray for? Why does he offer these prayers?

## Nehemiah Sent to Judah (2:1–8)

Nehemiah asked the king's permission to go to the exiles in Jerusalem to help with the rebuilding process. King Artaxerxes was gracious and granted his request.

SET THE SCENE

### A Big Building Project

The daunting task of rebuilding the walls around Jerusalem became Nehemiah's mission. God worked through the trust Nehemiah had built with Artaxerxes to receive the king's blessing, letters for safe passage, and permission to harvest timber from the king's forest to replace the gates of Jerusalem.

Nehemiah went out by night to inspect the city walls because he didn't want anyone to know what he planned to do until he knew the scope of work required. Why is it important for us to "do our homework" and prayerfully consider how to accomplish the work God has set before us? How do you balance reliance on God with putting in your own hard work for projects in your life?

## Nehemiah Inspects Jerusalem's Walls (2:9–20)

VISUALIZE

When he arrived in Jerusalem, Nehemiah began making plans to rebuild the once-great city's walls. He began the process by going alone at night to examine the current condition of the walls in order to determine the best course of action.

Nehemiah's skill for organization is shown as the work to repair the walls begins. How does God use the gifts He gave you to benefit others?

## Rebuilding the Wall (3:1–32)

Construction of the gates and walls begins after Nehemiah completes initial planning. Nehemiah makes a record of the process, detailing who rebuilt each structure and its location. The detailed records recount every section of wall and every gate.

## Opposition to the Work (4:1–14)

### VISUALIZE

When the project was underway and progressing well, antagonists rose up and invented schemes to derail the work on Jerusalem's wall. Nehemiah was unfazed, however, and encouraged prayer for God's guidance and protection from their enemies.

## The Work Resumes (4:15–23)

God answers Nehemiah's prayer and gives Judah the opportunity to build once again. He inspires them to work, armed and ready, knowing that He will fight on their behalf should someone seek to disrupt them.

## Nehemiah Stops Oppression of the Poor (5:1–13)

Nehemiah learns that the Judean nobles and officials are charging the poor Judeans excessive interest, which forces them to sell their children into slavery to foreigners in order to pay their debts. Nehemiah demands that the officials stop charging interest and restore the families and properties of their brothers.

Nehemiah fulfills God's will by correcting the unfair treatment of the poor. Who might take on that kind of responsibility in our world today? How can we help bring the needs of the poor to their attention?

## Nehemiah's Generosity (5:14–19)

During his tenure as governor of Judah, Nehemiah does not impose the crippling food allowance of his predecessors upon the Judeans. He dedicates his service wholly to rebuilding the city for God and not for any personal gain or advantage.

### PICTURE OF THE SAVIOR

**Nehemiah Leads the People**

When the people cried out for help, Nehemiah listened and, through his words and resources, rescued those who were oppressed and suffering.

Jesus rescues us from the oppression of sin and death through His life, death, and resurrection.

What is the value of a good name? When Nehemiah's enemies couldn't find a way to murder him, they attempted to assassinate his good name by spreading false information about him. Why is having a "good name" important? How do you respond when someone attacks your character?

## Conspiracy Against Nehemiah (6:1–14)

Even when construction on the wall nears its completion, the Judeans' enemies plot to derail Nehemiah's wise counsel with slander and false prophecy. Nehemiah remains firm and confident in God, trusting that the Lord will protect him from all manner of evil in his endeavor.

## The Wall Is Finished (6:15–7:4)

Judah finishes rebuilding its mighty wall in just fifty-two days, thanks to God's care and protection. Nehemiah designates God-fearing men to protect and maintain the walls in his stead.

## Lists of Returned Exiles (7:5–65)

Nehemiah records a census of Jerusalem in order to determine the remaining Judean bloodlines after the exile. He finds a ledger of the original exiles and adds it to his own for a more complete record.

## Totals of People and Gifts (7:66–73)

Nehemiah adds up the number of Judeans, their servants, their animals, and the treasures given to the city of Jerusalem.

Ezra read the Law of Moses to the people. The Law of Moses includes both Law and Gospel. Where do we hear the Law and Gospel read? Why is it important for us to hear and understand God's Law and His Gospel?

## Ezra Reads the Law (8:1–8)

The priest Ezra comes forward to read the Law of Moses to all the people who are gathered at the gate, including Judeans who were not believers. Nehemiah's work creates a wonderful venue for more to hear and believe the Word of God.

## This Day Is Holy (8:9–12)

Upon hearing the Word of God, many Judeans are sorrowful and weep as those convicted. Nehemiah, Ezra, and the other leaders are quick to bring God's promises of forgiveness, holiness, and redemption through celebration and feasting on the now sanctified day of His glory.

## LINK BETWEEN THE TESTAMENTS

**Ezra Reads the Law → Peter's Sermon at Pentecost (Nehemiah 8:1–12 → Acts 2:14–41)**

With the walls completed and the census taken, the priest Ezra read from the Law of Moses for six hours. Many were hearing the Law for the first time in their lives and they were cut to the quick. Ezra and the Levites reminded them that God had made that day holy, and they sent the people home to eat the riches the Lord provided and to rejoice in His promises and mercy.

A similar response happened on Pentecost when the apostle Peter preached a sermon recalling the life, death, and resurrection of Jesus Christ. Upon hearing this message, the people responded with grief, asking, "Brothers, what shall we do?" (Acts 2:37). Peter called on them to repent and be baptized, and three thousand responded to this call.

## Feast of Booths Celebrated (8:13–18)

As Ezra guides the Judeans in his teaching of God's Word, they read about the Feast of Booths, which they had neglected to celebrate. The assembly of believers quickly acts to rectify their ignorance and reestablish the Feast of Booths.

The Feast of Booths recalled Israel's wilderness wandering years and how God faithfully provided for all their needs. It later became a celebration of the harvest and God's generous gifts to His people. When do we celebrate God's generous gifts and harvest?

## SET THE SCENE

**Feast of Booths**

The weeklong Feast of Booths was one of the three annual festivals established by God through Moses in Exodus 23:16; 34:22. The people gathered leafy branches to create small shelters, or booths, in which families would "camp out" for the duration of the feast. These booths reminded the people of the wilderness wanderings, when Israel lived in tents and God provided for their needs and protected them.

## The People of Israel Confess Their Sin (9:1–38)

The former Judean exiles gather for a day of repentance to God for the many sins they were discovering as they studied the Scriptures. The praises they sing recount God's faithfulness and grace over the many years of His people's scorn.

The people gathered to repent of their sins. When do we gather to repent of our sins? Why is this important?

## The People Who Sealed the Covenant (10:1–27)

Nehemiah lists all the names of those who sealed the written document of the Judeans' commitment. The names are organized into distinct groups, starting with the officials, priests, Levites, and leaders.

## The Obligations of the Covenant (10:28–39)

Nehemiah also outlines the terms of the agreement for all the people to cling always to God in worship, praise, and deed.

### CLEAR THE CONFUSION

**What was the covenant Nehemiah made with Judea's leaders?**

Nehemiah gathered Judea's leaders to present a written covenant concerning God's expectations for His people. The covenant contained three clearly defined sections:

1. The Judeans should not intermarry with the local people to ensure God's people were not led away from Him to false gods.
2. The people were to remember the Sabbath day and the Sabbath year. The seventh day was dedicated to receiving the gifts of the true God, and the seventh year was dedicated to forgiveness and worship.
3. The final section of the covenant dealt with support for the temple, including financial support for the priests and Levites who served the temple.

## The Leaders in Jerusalem (11:1–24)

Nehemiah records the political proceedings necessary for Jerusalem's upkeep and defense. The leaders and one-tenth of the population stay in Jerusalem after casting lots.

## Villages Outside Jerusalem (11:25–36)

Nehemiah mentions that 90 percent of the Judeans will live beyond the city in the towns of the countryside.

At least 90 percent of the returned Judeans would live outside of Jerusalem. Why might it be important to have so many people living in small, rural towns? How does this compare to the distribution of the population today?

## Priests and Levites (12:1–26)

Nehemiah counts the priests and Levites from the time of the first wave of returned exiles to the time of the restoration of Jerusalem.

## Dedication of the Wall (12:27–43)

Now that the wall is finished, and before the returned exiles spread out across the land, Nehemiah leads a glorious dedication for the newly completed wall surrounding Jerusalem. The priests, musicians, choirs, and others march atop the wall in opposite directions.

The rededication of the wall in Jerusalem is cause for great celebration. When have you ever experienced a special service of dedication at your congregation or another place? What did you gain from that experience?

**VISUALIZE**

### Dedication Ceremonies

The dedication of the newly rebuilt wall in Jerusalem was a cause for great celebration among the people. After years in exile and finding Jerusalem in ruins, the people came together to restore and rebuild. The culmination of that effort resulted in the celebratory dedication parade atop the wall.

## Service at the Temple (12:44–47)

The day of dedication also sees assignments for the priests and Levites at the temple. Every area is addressed—and not one role is left unfilled—to restore the temple service to its days of preexilic glory.

**SET THE SCENE**

### The Silence of the Prophets

After the final Old Testament prophet, Malachi, a few years after Nehemiah's work, there would be a four-hundred-year silence from the prophets. Nehemiah had carefully set up guidelines for the long-term care and maintenance of the temple and the temple personnel. This organization would become invaluable during the long period of silence before Christ's appearance.

# Nehemiah's Second Visit: Problems and Solutions (13:1–31)

After returning to King Artaxerxes for some time, Nehemiah receives permission to go back to Jerusalem, where he finds problems that need to be resolved.

## Nehemiah's Final Reforms (13:1–31)

### WAYPOINT

***What does this text show us?***

Upon returning to Jerusalem, Nehemiah discovers the sinful behaviors and compromises that have set back in among the Judeans. Nehemiah recounts God's Law and sets things back to the way God would have them go.

***What does this text reveal about God's plan of salvation?***

God calls us away from our sinful actions to receive the gift of salvation won for us in the life, death, and resurrection of our Savior, Jesus Christ. We cannot turn the right way on our own; rather, the Holy Spirit works through Word and Sacrament to right our paths.

***What does this text uncover about our identity and calling as God's people today?***

God calls us to live our lives for Him in all that we do and say. Nehemiah's admonition to remain faithful to God's Word is a message to God's people today. We live our lives as God's children, following His direction for how we can use the gifts and talents He gives us to serve Him and one another.

Review the events of Nehemiah's second visit to Jerusalem. What highlights do you see in this section of the Scriptures?

How does God's plan of salvation work in our lives? How does He do all of the work in His plan?

What special gifts and talents has God given you? How can you use those gifts and talents to serve God and others?

### CLEAR THE CONFUSION

**Why did Nehemiah throw Tobiah out of the temple?**

Tobiah was a foreigner, an Ammonite. During the construction of the walls, Tobiah had been among the leaders who mocked the rebuilding of the walls (4:3). A priest who was related to him had cleared out space in the temple storage rooms for Tobiah. This event was related to the driving away of the foreign wives (with their children) who had married returned exiles.

## LINK BETWEEN THE TESTAMENTS

### Marriage Between Believers and Unbelievers (Nehemiah 13:23–27 → 1 Corinthians 7:12–16)

Nehemiah forcing Judean men to put away their foreign wives may seem harsh to us, but it was vital to protect the Judean community. They would have to endure intact through the intertestamental period—four hundred years in which they would face tremendous pressure to give up their distinctiveness and become like the other nations, especially like the Greek culture that came to dominate that part of the world for centuries.

Paul also spoke about mixed marriages between believers and unbelievers. God would have us avoid tying ourselves to someone who is not a believer. But for those already married to an unbeliever, Paul encouraged remaining in that marriage as long as the unbelieving spouse is willing, because God may work faith in the unbeliever through his or her Christian spouse. But if the unbelieving spouse seeks to leave the marriage because of the Christian's faith, then the believer is not bound in that marriage.

# ESTHER

## Welcome to Esther

The events in the book of Esther take place after the temple has been rebuilt in Jerusalem. A new threat is about to arise in the capital of the Persian Empire which will threaten the very existence of the Judeans and, thus, the line leading to the Savior of the world, Jesus Christ.

What do you know about the book of Esther? What are some specific things you'd like to learn more about?

## Esther at a Glance

- **Start:** The book of Esther begins with an extravagant, six-month-long banquet by the Persian king Ahasuerus.
- **End:** The book concludes with Queen Esther's cousin Mordecai managing the affairs of the Persian Empire.
- **Theme:** This book shows how God protects His people from powerful unbelievers who have no knowledge or fear of the Lord God.
- **Author and Date:** The author of Esther is unknown. It was likely composed around 400 BC.
- **Places Visited:** Susa, the capital city of Persia
- **Journey Time:** The ten chapters of Esther can be read in approximately half an hour.
- **Outline:**
  - Threat to Judeans (1:1–5:14)
  - Deliverance of Judeans (6:1–10:3)

## Five Top Sights and Spectacles of Esther

**The King's Banquet (1:1–22)** Join the lavish celebration of the king's banquet, which seems to have no end.

**Esther Chosen Queen (2:1–18)** See the king choose Esther from among all the other virgins in the kingdom to be his queen.

**Haman Plots Against Judeans (3:1–15)** Listen closely as Haman hatches his plot to destroy every single Judean.

**Esther Reveals Haman's Plot (6:14–7:8)** Feel the rage of the king as he sees Haman falling upon Esther after learning of Haman's plot to destroy her people.

**Judeans Destroy Enemies (9:1–19)** Range through the Persian Empire, watching the Judeans destroy the enemies who sought their extermination.

## Seeing Jesus in Esther

The absence of God's name throughout the entire book of Esther seems strange. But He is clearly at work behind the scenes, organizing everything for the good of His people. Can you name a situation in your life when God was guiding events for your good?

Though God's name is not used a single time in the entire text,we most clearly see Jesus in the Persian king Ahasuerus. He chooses an unlikely orphan girl as his queen, just as Christ Jesus chose sinners like us to be His Bride. When powerful enemies plot against Esther and her people, the king is filled with rage and commands their destruction. Jesus feels that same rage against the enemies of His church and will strike them with the rod of His mouth when He returns in judgment to bring us to live with Him in glory for an eternal banquet.

## Threat to Judeans (1:1–5:14)

The first section in Esther traces Esther's path to became queen of Persia and how a prominent official hatched a plot to destroy the Judeans.

### The King's Banquets (1:1–9)

In the third year of his reign, Persian king Ahasuerus holds a lavish, half-year banquet to celebrate his ascension to his father's throne. After this, he holds a weeklong banquet for the people in his citadel while his wife, Queen Vashti, holds her own banquet.

What is the longest banquet or celebration you have attended? What obstacles would you see in a celebration that lasted half of a year? What would it take to overcome those obstacles?

**PICTURE OF THE SAVIOR**

**An Everlasting Banquet**

Ahasuerus's feast lasted 180 days, nearly half of a year! Think of the eternal banquet we will celebrate with Jesus in the new heavens and the new earth. Jesus will lavish us with the most wonderful, amazing wedding banquet, as we celebrate His reign over all creation forever.

**SET THE SCENE**

**Who is Ahasuerus?**

Ahasuerus (486–465 BC) is also known by his Greek name, Xerxes. He was the son of Darius I (who authorized the returned exiles to complete the rebuilding of the temple) and great-grandson of Cyrus the Great (who issued the decree permitting the exiles to return to Jerusalem. *Ahasuerus* means "mighty man."

## Queen Vashti's Refusal (1:10–22)

On the last day of his second banquet, the king is drunk and wishes to parade his beautiful wife before his guests. Queen Vashti refuses. This enrages the king. After consulting his wise men, he banishes Vashti from his presence and intends to replace her with another.

## Esther Chosen Queen (2:1–18)

The king interviews young virgins to become his new queen. Esther, an orphaned Judean exile raised by her cousin Mordecai, wins the favor of the chief eunuch, and with his help wins the favor of the king. Ahasuerus selects Esther to be his queen and holds a great banquet in her honor.

Esther was surrounded by other beautiful young women who were all vying for the king's favor. How unlikely it must have seemed to Esther that the king would choose her, a poor, orphaned Judean girl. In what way are each of us Christians unlikely children of God?

## Mordecai Discovers a Plot (2:19–23)

Mordecai sits at the king's gate to learn news of Esther. He overhears an assassination plot by two eunuchs. Mordecai reports it to the king through Esther. An investigation finds the rumor to be true. The eunuchs are hanged, and Mordecai's service is recorded in the king's chronicles.

**SET THE SCENE**

**Assassination Plots**

In Old Testament times, kings employed cupbearers like Nehemiah to protect them from assassination. But as we saw with the kings of Israel and Judah, assassinations were not uncommon. In fact, King Ahasuerus would end up being assassinated by the captain of his bodyguard in a palace coup.

**The Gallows**

Esther 2:23 says the eunuchs who sought to assassinate Ahasuerus were "hanged on the gallows" (2:23). Persian gallows were long, sharp spikes on which victims were impaled and left to slowly die in great agony. The Romans got their idea for crucifixion from this mode of execution.

## Haman Plots Against the Jews (3:1–15)

**WAYPOINT**

Sometimes our enemies and adversaries are clear, while at other times we aren't aware we have any. What is your experience right now?

***What does this text show us?***

Five years after Mordecai exposes the assassination plot, Haman is promoted to the king's right hand. When Mordecai refuses to bow in Haman's presence, he discloses his Judean nationality. In prideful rage, Haman decides not to kill Mordecai alone but to annihilate every Judean throughout the Persian Empire.

***What does this text reveal about God's plan of salvation?***

Haman's desire to exterminate every Judean was ultimately induced by Satan. Jesus Himself faced that ancient hostility as He was put to death on the cross. But Jesus defeated Satan by making payment for all the sins of all people of all time.

How did Satan's plot to kill Jesus end up backfiring against him?

***What does this text uncover about our identity and calling as God's people today?***

We should not be surprised when we face deep hatred and persecution for the sake of Jesus. Just as we will see God's protection of Esther, Mordecai, and the people of Judea unfold in the coming chapters, we will also see His protection throughout our lives.

How have you seen God's protection in your life?

**SET THE SCENE**

**Who was Haman?**

Haman was an Agagite, which was a clan of the Amalekites, descendants of Jacob's brother, Esau. His hostility reflected the ancient hostility between the Edomites and Israelites (see 1 Samuel 15). That ancient hostility best explains his desire to annihilate all Judeans and not just Mordecai.

## Esther Agrees to Help the Jews (4:1–17)

When Mordecai reminds Esther she will not escape this edict, she agrees to risk her life to approach the king. She asks Mordecai to have all the Judeans in Susa fast and pray along with her for three days and nights first.

Esther knew her life would be at stake if she approached the king without first being summoned. She fasted and prayed for God to make the king's heart receptive to her. What is a situation in which you are asking God to turn someone's heart to be favorable to you?

## Esther Prepares a Banquet (5:1–8)

Esther risked her life by appearing uninvited in the royal court and approaching the king in her royal robes. Seeing Esther, the king extended his golden scepter to her in mercy. When the king promised to grant her request, up to half of his kingdom, Esther asked him to attend a private banquet for him and Haman. At the banquet, she requested that both of them come to another banquet the next day, at which she would present her request.

**PICTURE OF THE SAVIOR**

**Approaching Christ in Prayer?**

Many Christians hesitate to approach God's throne in prayer. Jesus welcomes us into His presence. He invites us, even commands us, to pray. This image of coming into the royal heavenly throne room and kneeling in front of Jesus to offer our prayer helps us be confident God will answer us favorably.

When have you been afraid to bring a deep concern to God in prayer? What made you fearful? Where can we find confidence to pray to God?

## Haman Plans to Hang Mordecai (5:9–14)

Haman leaves Esther's banquet in high spirits, until he sees Mordecai, who still refuses to bow or tremble in fear before him. He builds a gallows seventy-five feet high and the next morning approaches the king to discuss "having Mordecai hanged on the gallows" (6:4).

The Psalms often speak of enemies who have dug traps for us only to fall into the traps that they have dug (see Psalm 57:6). What comfort can you find when evildoers who trouble you seem to always be successful?

# Deliverance of Judeans (6:1–10:3)

The second part of the book of Esther shows how God works through Esther to deliver the Judeans, turn Haman's plot back on himself, and raise Mordecai to a prominent position in the kingdom from which he could look out for the benefit of the Judeans.

## The King Honors Mordecai (6:1–13)

The book of Esther does not directly mention God's name. How does the king's sleepless night point to God's "behind the scenes" intervention?

From a human point of view, Jesus' trials on Good Friday made it seem like Satan was in control. How did Jesus' resurrection on the third day uncover the truth?

It took nearly five years for Mordecai to be recognized for saving the king from assassination. How do you handle situations when your faithful actions are not recognized?

### WAYPOINT

***What does this text show us?***

When the king cannot sleep, he learns nothing was done to honor Mordecai for saving him from assassination. Just then, Haman enters the court to ask the king to execute Mordecai.

***What does this text reveal about God's plan of salvation?***

God protects His people. He makes Haman fall into the trap he had dug for Mordecai by arranging for a sleepless night for the king and for the account of Mordecai to be read from the chronicles of the kingdom.

***What does this text uncover about our identity and calling as God's people today?***

God watches over our lives with the same care and concern. He knows the plots of our enemies, and knows how to make our enemies fall into the very pit they dig for us. Entrusting our lives into God's protective care, we can boldly love our neighbor and share the good news of God's salvation.

## Esther Reveals Haman's Plot (6:14–7:6)

At the second banquet, Esther reveals that she is Judean and Haman has scheduled her people for extermination. Ahasuerus is outraged for the sake of his wife and by this shameful betrayal by his trusted minister.

## Haman Is Hanged (7:7–10)

In a rage, Ahasuerus stomps off into the palace garden to determine what to do. While he is gone, a terrified Haman bows before Esther, begging for his life. At that moment, the king returns to find what looks like Haman attacking Esther for exposing him. A eunuch points out the gallows Haman built the day before for Mordecai.

## Esther Saves the Jews (8:1–17)

The king gives Haman's house and property to Esther and gives Haman's position to Mordecai. Esther pleads for the king to revoke Haman's murderous edict. Though it can't be revoked, the king directs Mordecai to proclaim another law to counteract Haman's devilish decree.

### CLEAR THE CONFUSION

**Why couldn't the laws of the Persians be altered or revoked?**

The Persians believed their emperors were gods. Since they were gods, they would never make mistakes that needed to be altered. The Bible claims the same about the words God spoke through His prophets and apostles. The Scriptures are incapable of having errors because the Holy Spirit inspired every word. Since God is unchanging and omniscient, His Word never changes.

Our world is always changing, and so is our culture and the people around us. We are always changing too. Why is it an advantage to us that God never changes? How does that truth comfort you today?

### PICTURE OF THE SAVIOR

**Mordecai**

In the Old Testament, Mordecai became the third Israelite exalted to the right hand of a ruler and given all authority throughout that kingdom. First was Joseph under Pharaoh in Egypt (Genesis 41:37–44). Then Daniel ruled under Darius the Mede in Persia (Daniel 6:3, 28). Now Mordecai would govern under

Ahasuerus in Persia. Each of these men prefigured Jesus' exaltation, where He sits at the right hand of God the Father, ruling all creation for the benefit of His Bride, the church.

## The Jews Destroy Their Enemies (9:1–19)

On the day when Haman and the enemies of the Judeans had hoped to crush them, the Judeans gain the upper hand. Officials throughout Persia fear Mordecai's growing power and assist the Judeans.

### CLEAR THE CONFUSION

**How could God be pleased with the His people slaughtering so many of their enemies?**

Three times in this text we read the phrase "but they laid no hand on the plunder" (see vv. 10, 15–16). This slaughter by the Judeans was never about their own personal gain or vengeance. It was strictly for protection, to eliminate the enemies who sought their elimination.

## The Feast of Purim Inaugurated (9:20–32)

Mordecai and Esther write letters inaugurating an annual festival called Purim. *Purim* is the Hebrew word for "lots." This festival is named for the lots Haman had cast to fix the date for the annihilation of the Judeans. This festival will recall how God turned Haman's plot against him and rescued the Judeans from annihilation.

## The Greatness of Mordecai (10:1–3)

Mordecai rises in power to be second to the king, seeking the welfare of his people and speaking peace to them all—similar to Jesus Christ at the Father's right hand, calming us and speaking peace through His Gospel.